Published by Dr. Jean-Jacques D'Aoust

Loveland, Colorado

Available at Amazon.com

ISBN-13:   978-1511631655
ISBN-10: 1511631651

Apology for a Monk in the World

Reverend Father Jean-Jacques D'Aoust, Ph.D., OSBOblate

Dedicated to my Father, Henri D'Aoust (1886-1934)

And Mother, Aurore Theriault-Labrosse (1892-1981)

"I have loved you with an everlasting love,

I have drawn you with unfailing kindness."
Jeremiah 31:3

"An unexamined life is not worth living."
Socrates

Apology for a Monk in the World

When I first became a monk in 1947, I read, meditate, willingly and faithfully followed all that the Rule of Saint Benedict required. Unfortunately, my loyalty eventually faltered. I now want to heal the harm I have done in my life and return to the Lord. Despite my failings, He has never abandoned me but instead, like the prodigal Father, has blessed me generously throughout my life and delivered me from many troubles. So long as we live, and no matter how badly we stumble, it is never too late to return to the road of salvation. Thus—on with the journey!

Many friends, relatives, and sympathizers have repeatedly urged me to write an autobiography to record some of the fortunate as well as the disastrous experiences I have had up to my 90th birthday. An appropriate title would be: <u>An Apology for the Life of a Monk in the World</u>.

In 1947 1 entered and lived for nine years in the strictly cloistered and contemplative monastery of Saint-Benoit-du-Lac, near Magog, in the province of Quebec. Then, in 1956, 1 transferred to the active Archabbey of St. Vincent, in Latrobe, Pennsylvania. The story of those sixteen years of monastic life will be told later on. Then, in 1963, I left both the Roman Catholic Church and the monastic life to become an Episcopalian. Most recently, on October 26, 2014, I became an Oblate of St. Walburga Abbey, in Virginia Dale, Colorado. I am back with an affiliation with the Order of Saint Benedict.

Family Influences

I found out that my ancestors came from Picardie, a province north of Paris, in 1686, and settled on the island of Montreal. They were silk merchants. From Montreal the family spread out, mostly as merchants.

My grandfather, Felix D'Aoust was an architect and builder who specialized in constructing churches. Since this is not a regular occurrence, he was often unemployed. I remember him smoking a long, white pipe, sitting in front of my father's store, and talking to everyone who passed by. Fortunately, his wife was a successful seamstress and the main wage-earner for the family of four children.

My father, Henri D'Aoust, was born in 1866, in Alfred, Ontario. He was his parents' first child. He wanted to become a priest, but his family could not afford to send him to college. At 17, after graduation from high school, he went to work for his uncle, who ran a grocery store in Kirkland Lake, Ontario. In eight years, he saved enough money to buy the only general store of his native village. At twenty-five, he married Aurore Thériault-Labrosse, then only 18, and she eventually became my mother. Her own father, Paul Thériault, a grocer in Montreal, died when she was a month old. Her widowed mother, Lumina Ricard, re-married a wealthy widower farmer, Wilfrid Labrosse, who owned several farms. He had five sons, to two of whom he gave a complete farm. Another became a carpenter and building contractor; a fourth became the owner of several shoe stores in Montreal, and the fifth became a day laborer.

My mother wanted to become a nun, like many of her cousins and aunts. However, her parents would not allow that. They wanted to keep her at home to entertain their guests. She was very fortunate to receive a very good musical education. At the beginning of the twentieth century, in France, a law was passed to abolish all religious organizations. That left only one option for the French nuns who were facing dissolution of their order; they could go as missionaries to one of their current or former colonies. Thus, four displaced nuns from Paris-one with a doctorate in music from the Sorbonne- traveled across the Atlantic to Ontario, Canada, and the little village of Alfred-population 1,5000.

The nun with the doctorate became my mother's mentor and taught her to play piano professionally. Mother was given a piano when she was only ten years old and she played it until the year she died at 89, in 1981. She would play in church, as well as at her parents' parties, that consisted of singing folk songs and dancing. I still remember when my younger brother André and I were small and Mother would put us in bed at night and then sit at the piano and play. We fell asleep listening to Chopin, Brahms, Liszt, Schumann, and others. Sometimes even today, tears come to my eyes when I hear this music played on a piano. Those are beautiful memories…and how wonderful to have them!

My oldest sister, Marie-Rose, graduated from college, taught grade school for many years, became a nun among the Sisters of St Anne, a French Canadian congregation. She became known as Sister Marie-Rose-de-la-Trinité. After earning master's degrees in education and psychology, she was promoted to principal of a female junior college. This college became coeducational in 1960, and the nuns had to resume secular clothing; this was required by Vatican II and the secularization of education in Quebec. All these changes disturbed very much Marie-Rose.

At 65, she had a stroke, became paralyzed, and lost the ability to speak. After two years, she relearned to speak, at first, the skill to articulate words, as her left Broca's area healed, and then the ability to discern the meaning of words, when her Wernicke area healed. She was able to attend courses at the University of Montreal, on the history and critique of movies. This enabled her to give some lectures on the movies. Marie-Rose was a great influence in my life; from my early studies, she monitored and stimulated my intellectual curiosity. She died of a stroke at 75.

At my baptism, Marie-Rose, at age 12, was my godmother and my oldest brother, Paul-Emile, at age 10, became my godfather. At that time, Mother made a vow that she would do anything to enable me to become a priest.

My oldest brother also wanted to become a priest. However, in junior high, a hockey accident injured his left leg and developed a blood poisoning. He was a month in coma. When he recovered, he had lost his short term memory. Although he studied very hard, his memory was blank when the examinations came. His academic studies were interrupted and he became a religious brother of the Oblates of Mary Immaculate.

It was he who gave me my first Bible and taught me how to read it. His great love of the Immaculate Conception was an inspiration for me. Musically gifted, he played piano and organ very well. He liked to improvise and would spend hours doing just that. When the whole family would go on a Sunday drive, he preferred to stay home to play the piano. He told endless humorous stories, like his grandmother. He was put in charge of the printing business of the

Oblates of Mary Immaculate. He died of a stroke at 69.

My second sister, Thérèse, became a registered nurse and worked in surgery. She was a very beautiful blond girl. Young doctors would court her; but my mother insisted they do that in our parlor; and at 10 pm, she would tell the doctor that it was time to leave. Obviously, Thérèse never married. Later, she went to the Nursing School of the Catholic University in Washington, D.C., and earned a master's degree in nursing education. She taught in a nursing school in Montreal, and later, became head of the psychiatric nursing department in a Montreal hospital. At 65, she retired and planned to go skiing. Unfortunately, she slipped, fell on ice outside her apartment, and broke her hip. She was in a wheelchair for the rest of her life.

With another psychiatric nurse, Marion Hagedoorn, they bought a house and shared it. The family of Marion was prisoners of war by the Japanese for four years, in Indonesia. Her father had been an exporter of wood from Indonesia to Holland. The mother died in concentration camp; Marion at 8 years old took care of her two younger brothers, while the father was in a different camp. After liberation, they all went back to Holland and then decided to immigrate to Canada. For the last two years of her life, Thérese was committed to a nursing home, with Marion, her friend, coming in daily to offer some physical exercises, medication, and companionship. She died at 92.

My youngest sister, Marie-Antoinette, graduated from college, taught elementary school for many years, and married George Gill, a former seminarian. Since they married late, they could not have children of their own; so, they adopted, first a girl, Jocelyne; then a boy, Pierre. Jocelyne never graduated from high school, because of problems with alcohol and drugs.

Pierre graduated from high school, after which he drove his motorcycle to Banff, in British Columbia, to work for a year as a waiter in the hotel. There, he became interested in photography, and came back to the University of Montreal, to graduate in film making. At this time, he has over 30 films to his credit, many earning several honors in Canada. From his first wife he had two children, Mathys and Dali; from his second wife, Julie, he has a baby, Laura Jane.

When I emailed him recently, he was in Budapest, doing another filming.

At age 54, when André got married, Mother, with no more family obligations, decided to realize her life ambition to become a nun. She entered a strictly cloistered and contemplative monastery in Hull, Quebec. She found herself in the novitiate with teen aged girls. For spiritual direction, they were studying the catechism. Since Mother had read a lot of philosophy and theology, she was not much inspired by this very elementary teaching. They were teaching her how to fold her hands and how to genuflect. When André came to visit her with his little baby girl, Mother could see the baby only through a barred window and could not touch the baby. Mother thought that inhuman. When a man was in the courtyard, a young nun could not go out except accompanied by an older nun. Mother would say to younger nuns all men are not wolves; your father was not a wolf. After running a business, Mother had problems with obedience and silence. After a year she decided to leave, finding the rules antiquated. While she had been going to church daily to receive communion, after her monastic experience she refused to go to church anymore.

My oldest sister, Marie-Rose, a nun, brought to Mother every Sunday a pix with seven consecrated hosts, which Mother kept on top of her piano with a vigil lamp in front, and gave herself communion every day. Yet, she was still reading a lot of Scripture and spiritual theology. She would write me and her rector some 14-page letters in which she paraphrased some passages of St. Paul. At her funeral in her parish church, the Pastor allowed me to concelebrate, even though I was now an Episcopal priest, and read some of Mother's letters to him in lieu of an homily. Mother has always been a great inspiration in my life by her patience, perseverance, compassion, prayer life, and love.

Marie-Antoinette lived on the second floor of her three floor apartment building. Her daughter, Jocelyne lived on the ground floor; she died of ill health two years ago. Her son Pierre lived on the third floor when he was in town. He was often out of town, to do some filming. So, when Marie-Antoinette, at age 91, fell twice in her apartment, with no one to help her, Pierre made his move. He placed her in an independent living arrangement residence, Chateau Vincent d'Indy, in Montreal. At first, she became very depressed, since, against her will, she had been taken from her home of some 35 years. When I spoke to her on the phone, I thought she was dying. I flew immediately to Montreal to visit with her. Pierre got a physical therapist to come daily, to get her out of bed and to the dining room, and a nurse to come weekly, to check on her physical condition. I went back to Montreal for her 92d birthday, on August 11, 2013, and her 93rd birthday, in 2014. The last time I talked to her on the phone, she sounded in very good mood. I thank God for that. I called her today, March 25,2015, to find out that she is suffering from a bad lower denture. I emailed her son, Pierre, who happened to be in Budapest, informed him of his mother's situation. He promised to take care of her immediately.

My father was a successful businessman with his general store in Alfred, Ontario, selling food, clothing, furniture, and farm equipment to farmers, who sometimes had no cash. They would then barter: eggs, vegetables, chickens, pigs, or even once a cow, which mother would milk every morning. With our maternal parents living nearby, we did very well. I remember a time when the convent next to the church burned down. I watched it from the living room window of our house across the street. The five nuns, with no place to go, were sheltered in our home.

When Cornwall, Ontario, in 1927, became a boom town with a new textile plant moving in, my father thought it opportune to take advantage of the situation. He began building a department store there and sold his business in Alfred. We lived on the third floor above the store.

During the Depression, my father sold often on credit: food, clothing, and furniture to hundreds of families which were unemployed. Several of his friends committed suicide when they lost all their fortune. Father was very generous. I remember during the period of Advent when collections were made for the poor, Father would empty many shelves of clothing from his store to give to the poor. I remember well on Sundays during the summer when Father, who played the cornet in the municipal band, would play in neighboring towns in the afternoon. After the family picnic, the whole family would drive back home, while Father and Mother were saying the rosary in the front seat, and the children were falling asleep in the back. Meanwhile, father was getting terrible headaches. Doctors would say that he was working too much, and recommended rest in a sanatorium for several months. Mother would take care of the store.

After the Depression, she hired a collecting agency to deal with our debtors. When she found that agency was defrauding her, Mother took over the collection of debts. Only to find out that some families which owed us several thousands of dollars could pay only 25 cents a week. Mother became discouraged and burned the bills. She sold the store and moved the family to Ottawa, near colleges and the University of Ottawa.

She took a nine bedroom house which she turned into a boarding house, with six bedrooms rented to boarders for room and board. In addition, she offered home-cooked meals to twelve university students. Two of my older siblings were boarders in local colleges. That means she prepared daily meals for six boarders, twelve university students and four children at home. Her day began at 4am; she stoked the coal furnace, prepared the breakfasts, and went to daily Mass. Her spiritual advisor was the assistant rector of the local Sacred Heart Church, who was a Jansenist, the equivalent of a Puritan.

He recommended that Mother make a vow of celibacy, as the early Christian widows, attend Mass daily, have regular evening prayers with the family, spend daily time for reading the Scripture and private meditation.   I followed Mother's example and developed a spiritual experience with God.

I attended daily Mass with Mother and often served as an acolyte. The pastor of the local Sacred Heart Church, Father Lionel Scheffer, asked me to visit the shut-ins he would be visiting the following week, in order to inform them of his visit ahead of time. That provided me with an opportunity to visit the shut-ins and begin to exercise some form of pastoral ministry.

Father took a turn for the worse.   A surgeon came from New York City to Ottawa, and diagnosed a brain tumor in the cerebellum. That would explain why Father was losing his equilibrium, even his speech, and walked as if he were drunk.   The surgical intervention was scheduled for a Monday.   Prior to that, Mother sent Marie-Antoinette, André and I to live with our grandparents in Alfred, for the weekend.   I did not sleep well on Saturday night.   Waking up early on Sunday morning, I went to the eight o'clock Mass, only to hear the priest announce from the pulpit that Henri D'Aoust had died the previous night, on August 4, 1934, the eighth birthday of my brother André; I was ten years old. That stunned me; he was my father.

I remained in a daze for over a month. Eventually, I often experienced daydreaming, even in class. I remember the incident in my last year of elementary school when the lay male teacher asked me some questions, and receiving no answer, he said that I was not very intelligent and would not even graduate from the first grade of high school. I vowed he would be wrong. I studied so hard in that first year, that I got A-grades and won a silver medal. Mother told me that my father was now in heaven. I identified him with God the Father. That thought was a constant reminder of how much God loves me.

My younger brother, André, was accident-prone from the very beginning of his life. At one, he broke his knee while doing somersaults in bed. At two, when he opened the door of the apartment we lived in, three floors above the store, there was no floor; he fell down on a tool box. At three, he fell down from a broken branch of a tree while pretending to be Tarzan. At four and a half, he burned a third of his skin while playing with matches. Mother heard his cries from the store she was managing and ran to put out the fire with her bare hands. The doctor said that André would not survive. Mother preferred to take care of him at home for a year and a half.

When he began to heal, the new skin forcing him to bend forward, she placed a broom behind his back under his arms to straighten him out. When he was 8, Mother had problems to discipline him. If he was angry with Mother, he would climb some 60 feet in trees behind our house, where he had placed a platform between two of them, and then sit there on a rocking chair for hours with the cat he picked up off the street. Mother, who grew up on a farm, thought that all animals belonged in the barn. In spite of Mother's calling, André remained unmoved. Mother had to call the police. She realized she needed a man to discipline André.

So, in the last year of his grade school, she placed him as a boarder in the prep school, a block from home. She required that I too would be a boarder, so as to keep watch over my younger brother. André had to walk only four blocks to his elementary school. The Oblates of

Mary Immaculate, who ran the prep school, took care of André's physical development. He became excellent in many sports: basketball, tennis, and hockey. He made the first team in his junior and senior hockey varsity teams. He could have been a professional hockey player, had several offers, but Mother would not sign the release forms. In spite of that, André was always very grateful for what Mother had done for him.

During World War II, all men 19 years old and up had to enlist in a military service. I joined the Naval Training Division of the Royal Canadian Navy in 1943 till 1945. During the academic year, I would attend regular university classes, with basic training three evenings a week. During June, July and August, I served on active duty from the naval base of Annapolis Royal, near Digby, Nova Scotia. We patrolled North Atlantic, looking for German submarines. We did not find any, but we found many whales. During the winter months, a military hockey league was formed in Ottawa: three army teams, three air force teams, all made up with former professional hockey players; and one navy team, made up exclusively of university students. I played defense, although I had never made the varsity team of the University of Ottawa. André had joined the University Naval Training Division also and played center. He was the top scorer for the senior varsity team of the University of Ottawa. We lost every game against the professionals, but André scored at least once in every game. He was a very fast skater.

André grew tired of riding his bicycle five miles, up and down hills to the New Edinburg Tennis Club, where we played tennis and swam. The club house was built on the Ottawa River and could be reached by a foot bridge. On land there were 21 tennis courts. André borrowed $60 from our sister, Thérèse, and bought a 1919 McLaughlin-Buick. It was a relic. It went very well on flat roads; but, climbing hills was a problem. He found out that in reverse the car could make it. He kept a bottle of bolts to stick in the wheels of the gears when they slipped.
When his tennis team played another tennis team on the other side of town, André took 14 players in his car.

There was place only for four passengers: in the driver seat; in a stool swiveling out from beneath the dash board; in a little reset beside the driver seat there was a bench for two passengers. Of the fourteen players, some sat inside, others on top of them, some on the running boards, some on the trunk. When they won their match, they came back to the New Edinburg Club to celebrate. The celebration lasted through the night. At midnight, they got into the car and drove through the expensive neighborhood, near Rideau Hall, the home of the Governor General, and tooted their horns. Of course, they were arrested and Mother saw the police report in the morning newspaper. Mother was ashamed of her son causing so many traffic violations. One day, when André was in school, she called a dump truck and demanded them to haul the car to the dump. When André returned from school, he was very angry and disappeared from home for two weeks. I searched for him and found him living with some friends and brought him back home.

André dropped out of college in his freshman year because he was playing too many sports. Mother told him to go to work. He got a job with the civil service in Ottawa, got married, went back to evening school, and graduated with a B.A. He found teaching English and mathematics in a junior college, in Rouyn, Québec. After a while, he became an editor of the local newspaper; then editor of trade journals, and finally, director of the Board of Real Estate for the province of Québec. In this capacity, he planned and organized courses in real estate in several colleges. Several national and international conferences for real estate were organized by André. From his first wife, he had 5 children: Jeanne, who married a member of the police force of Montreal, later a United Nations peace officer in Haiti. They were divorced and Jeanne is now living in Montreal. Roch went to college in Florida, on a tennis scholarship, graduated as an accountant, opened his accounting firm in Panama City, had two children, and is now retired in Florida. Suzanne graduated as an electronic engineer. She is now a commercial artist in Vancouver. Jean graduated as a civil engineer, was married, has a daughter and is now a financial advisor in Montreal. Marc graduated from law school and opened his own law firm in St. Jerome. He was married, had three children, but died a few years ago.

After André retired from his real estate work, at age 57, he married his executive secretary, Marthe, who was 20 years younger. With her, he had two more boys, Robert, who became an architect, and Patrick, who became a professional baseball player, until a concussion forced him to change from playing to coaching.

When these two boys were born, André wanted them to be baptized, but the priest would not do it because of his divorce. From then on, André would not speak to any priest. André and all his boys played tennis all their lives. When he retired, he and his wife moved to Fort Myers in the winter, and remained in Riviere Beaudette for the summer.

At 75, he was required to take a physical examination to renew his driving license. The doctor put him in the hospital because of an enlarged prostate. He was then on kidney dialysis for eight years before he died at 83. He had 7 children, 10 grandchildren and 10 great grandchildren. The great love that his children and grandchildren had for André was a consolation for him, in contrast to the neglect I have experienced from my own two sons.

Early academic education

After elementary school, I entered the bilingual prep school of the University of Ottawa. We called that prep school: *le cours d'immatriculation*. After four years in the prep school, I entered the college department of Arts. The first two years were called: *Belles-Lettres* and *Rhétorique* = Humanities. I enjoyed very much my studies, especially reading the literature of the great French authors: Moliere, La Fontaine, Racine, Corneille, Rabelais, Hugo, Peguy, Verlaine, Bloy, Mauriac, Claudel, and others. We did read some British authors: Shakespeare, Milton. Blake, More, Tennyson, and some American authors: Cooper, Twain, Whitman, Irving, Poe. Reading poetry aloud was a favorite past-time; unfortunately I never developed the skill of writing poetry. In science I studied mathematics, algebra, trigonometry, physics, chemistry, biology, and psychology.

Books that I read then which formed my intellectual outlook were principally from four authors: Father Gratry. Les Sources; A.D. Sertillanges: La Vie Intellectuelle; Alexis Carrel, L`Homme, cet Inconmnu; Pierre Termier, La Joie de Connaitre.

Two of the philosophical principles of Father Gratry were the following:
1) search the truth with all your soul: all your emotions, all your intelligence, and all your moral character;

2) all things have been created by God and all truth depends on God. That was said under the influence of St. Augustine.

Recently, I found an English translation of the book of Sertillanges I read some 72 years ago, which inspired all my life. In answer to the question: ``Do you want to do intellectual work?`` he wrote: "Begin by creating within you a zone of silence, a habit of recollection, a will to renunciation and detachment which puts you entirely at the disposal of work; acquire that state of soul unburdened by desire and self-will which is the state of grace of the intellectual worker. Without that you will do nothing, at least nothing worthwhile."

Pierre Termier, a French geologist, came to the United States to explore the Grand Canyons. He described his experiences in his book, La Joie de Connaitre (1928), in such beautiful poetic language that it inspired me very much for the joy of learning.

Alexis Carrel was born in 1873, in Sainte-Foy-les-Lyon, France, and educated at the University of Lyon where he obtained his doctorate in medicine. He was a pioneer in transplant ology and thoracic surgery. In 1902, he witnessed officially the miraculous cure of Marie Bailly at Lourdes. After the notoriety surrounding the event, Carrel could not obtain a hospital appointment because of the anti-clericalism in the French university system at the time. In 1903 he emigrated to Montreal, Canada; then to Chicago, and finally to the Rockefeller Institute of Medical Research in New York, where he spent the rest of his life. With Charles Lindberg he built the first perfusion pump used in the development of organ transplantation and open heart surgery.

In 1935, Carrel wrote a book entitled, "L'Homme, cet Inconnu, which became a best seller. The book discussed his social prescriptions, advocating that mankind could better itself by following the guidance of an elite group of intellectuals. Well aware of the unceasing development of new scientific research, he suggested that from now on scientists and scholars of all disciplines should gather and work together for a better cooperation in scientific research. That became a dream for me, which unfortunately I never realized. Years later, I found that Ken Wilber had the same dream and is actually realizing this dream with his *Integral Institute*, of which I will speak later.

Later on, I took the Myers Briggs personality test. I seemed to fit the INTJ personality type. Such persons are analytical problem-solvers, eager to improve systems and processers with their innovative ideas. They have a talent for seeing possibilities for improvement, whether at work, at home, or in themselves. Often intellectual, INTJs enjoy logical reasoning and complex problem-solving. They approach life by analyzing the theory behind what they see, and are typically inward, on their own thoughtful study of the world around them. INTJs are drawn to logical systems and are much less comfortable with the unpredictable nature of other people and their emotions. They are typically independent and selective about their relationships, preferring to associate with people who they find intellectually stimulating.

My dream was to study philosophy, theology, medicine and then join a group of scholars from various disciplines. After the Humanities, I decided to take a more intense course of philosophy. Instead of the regular two years of philosophy in the department of Arts, I joined the Institute of Philosophy and took some more intensive courses with mostly seminarians.

Many of the courses were taught exclusively in Latin. By that time, I could read, write and speak Latin as a second language. The Institute of Philosophy was about three miles from home. I remember very well the long philosophical discussions I had with my two friends, Jean-Paul Bazinet and Jean-Paul Binet, on street corners on our way home. After my graduation with B.A. and B.Ph., I registered in the school of medicine of the University of Ottawa. The dean happened to have been a friend of my father.

The summer before beginning of the academic year I was strongly arm-twisted to take over the leadership of the Catholic University Students association for the diocese of Ottawa. I went to a leadership training camp on the island of St. Paul, in the middle of Richelieu River. There I met several university students from the Universities of Montreal and of Laval, in Quebec, several of whom later became important provincial and federal officers, like prime minister, ambassador, or even General Governor of Canada. I feared the responsibilities that would take too much time from the medical studies. Consequently, before the end of the week, I got in a row boat and rowed back to shore. Half way across I had something like the Damascus experience of St. Paul. I broke down crying and felt I was wrestling with God. Finally, I surrendered and committed myself to a new form of ministry.

During that first year of medical school I would study from 6am till 2am, biochemistry, anatomy and physiology, and spend several weekends visiting high schools and colleges to recruit natural leaders to form cells of Catholic University Students. I met Jacqueline Desjardins, who was the chairman of the female branch of the CUS. At that time, male and female activities were kept separate in the French branch of the Roman Catholic Church. Jacqueline was a top student in her senior year of college. She played piano like my mother and our two families got along very well.

We read together many books, including Les Grandes Amitiées, of Raissa Maritain. To a generation that needed to hear it, Raissa gave an account of the hope that was within her and did so with the gentleness and reverence. As a chronicle of the Catholic revival in France, her books were without equal. More than this, however, they offer us nothing less than a theology of conversion and Christian vocation expressed in a narrative that traces the effects of God's mercy upon the lives of a generation searching for meaning. For anyone who may be tempted to doubt God's enduring love for his wayward people, these books continue to offer hope for troubled times.

I found out later that after World War I, Jacques and Raissa with her sister Vera became Benedictine oblates, establishing together a domestic community of prayer and study. Jacques and Raissa had decided to live as brother and sister, forsaking marital intimacy and the joys of raising a family in order to dedicate themselves more deeply to their vocation to serve the truth. It was also during those years that the Maritains discovered Thomas Aquinas and began, under the guidance of their Dominican mentors, to study his works in depth. Their life dedicated to the pursuit of truth wherever you can find it and their entertainment of several scholars and scientists became a dream that inspired Jacqueline Desjardins and me, - not their vow of celibacy while being married.

When I began working as the chairman of the Catholic University Students, that time was when the Vatican recommended a greater participation of lay people in the ministry of the Church. To my surprise, I found rectors of parishes jealous of their authority and suspicious of lay participation. I became somewhat anti-clerical, at least towards priests who feared lay people active in ministry. I found out that the priests in the French Canadian parishes were too much domineering. That aspect of the priesthood was alien to me and at that time I preferred to dedicate myself to lay ministry.

After the final examinations of the first year of medicine, I decided to make a vocational retreat. My brother, Paul-Emile, suggested that I come to one of their retreat centers, the Oblates of Mary Immaculate. I knew they produced mainly parish priests and missionaries. That did not interest me at the time. Jean-Paul Bazinet suggested that I go to the Abbaye de Saint-Benoit-du-Lac, near Magog, in the province of Quebec.

I arrived there on the eve of Pentecost 1947. When I heard the choral recitation of the divine office, the organ playing, and the Gregorian chant, I thought I was in heaven. The next morning I asked for an interview with the Abbot and asked him if I could enter the monastery. He asked me: "How long have you thought of that?" I responded, "Since yesterday." He said: "Come back in August and make a week long retreat and then we will decide."

During the summer I organized two summer camps for leaders of the Catholic University Students in the diocese of Ottawa: one for high school students and one for university students, with Mother and my three sisters as cooks. In August 1947, I went back to Saint Benoit-du-Lac to make my vocational retreat. Mother decided to come with me. While I was praying to enter the monastery, Mother was praying that instead of entering the monastery I would enter a seminary to become a parish priest. She thought that entering a monastery was a flight from ministering to the people. I thought that monks pray for people all the time. I decided to enter the monastery.

I returned home and told Jacqueline my decision to become a monk. Jacqueline broke down crying. I asked her why? She said: "Because I love you." I said: "I do too, but I feel that God is calling me." We went to church, prayed together and made our sacrifice. Later, I learned from Mother that Jacqueline waited five

years, until I made solemn vows, before she
decided to marry a friend of mine, who was a
lawyer. Later, in moments of depression, I had
second thoughts about my religious vocation. If I
had been told that it was not my vocation, I
would gladly have left the monastery, returned to
the medical school, specialize in psychiatry and
then marry Jacqueline.

Abbaye de Saint Benoit-du-Lac

www.shutterstock.com · 99466379

On September 7, 1947, I
entered the Abbaye of Saint-Benoit-du-Lac
and did two years of novitiate, during
which time I learned a lot about the history
of monasticism, spirituality, liturgy and

Sacred Scripture. Then, two years of philosophy, even though I already had a B.Ph. Very soon, I was appointed the infirmarian of the monastery. According to the Rule of Saint Benedict: "Care of the sick must rank above all else so that they may truly be served as Christ who said: "I was sick and you visited me." We had 100 monks, about 50 lay workers in the farm and cheese factory, and an average of 50 male guests every day. Later on, I was put in charge of the kitchen. For this work, I was sent to a hospital in Montreal to take a course in dietetics. I was able to develop a month in advance the menu for three meals a day, seven days a week, taking in consideration the various dietetic needs of several monks. With all this responsibility, I enjoyed all the choir services, the philosophical and theological studies. Every morning, I was eager to get to the chapel, not only for my devotion to God, but also selfishly because our bedroom was not heated while the chapel was. I have always been cold in my life and savored the warmth of the chapel, while praying was warmth to my heart.

I was never asked to read alone in the chapel or during meals in the refectory. I wondered why? I was told several times, that I should not sing any louder than anyone else, never let my voice pierce from the group. I supposed there was a problem with my voice, or perhaps with my pronunciation. I was the only monk who came from bilingual Ontario, while the majority of monks were from the province of Quebec. I supposed they had a better pronunciation. Eventually, I was given voice lessons, both at Saint-Benoit-du-Lac, and at St Vincent Archabbey. During meals, both at noon and in the evening, there was always someone reading from some history books, philosophy, theology, spirituality, history. We learned a lot in this fashion, while eating in silence.

I remember that the history of the popes by Louis Pastor was read; we heard from the good and the bad popes; it was not always very uplifting. His approach was that the apparent shortcomings of the papacy have reflected flaws of their times. The series was contained in 16 volumes from the time of the Avignon Papacy of 1305 to Napoleon`s entrance in Rome, 1799.

I wanted to study Hebrew, but no one knew Hebrew in the monastery. I found a Latin grammar in the library for the study of Hebrew. Fortunately, some years later, I was lucky to meet a monk who spoke fluently Hebrew.

This was Johannan Weinhoven, a Dutch monk who entered the German Monastery in Jerusalem. For fear that Jews would seek some revenge against the Germans for their persecution during World War II, the German monks came in turn to spend some years in their foundation in Connecticut, to obtain American citizenship, hoping this would provide them security in Jerusalem. Thus, Johannan came to Mount Savior in Connecticut, and from there, spent some months at Saint Benoit-du-Lac. He became my Hebrew mentor. After he returned to Jerusalem, he took a few courses from Martin Buber at the University of Jerusalem. Through his biblical studies, he came to reject the divinity of Jesus. He left the monastery, sold his monastic habit, bought some secular clothing, found employment as a cook on a slow freighter sailing to New York City, got a job cooking in a restaurant, obtained a scholarship to Brandeis University, studied the Jewish religion, became a rabbi, got his Ph.D., and taught at Smith College, in Massachusetts.

Before I began my studies of theology, in 1952, I was required to swear on my knees the *Anti-Modernist oath* required by Pius X, since 1910, from all candidates to the ministry. This took half an hour to read in Latin. I found out that Pius IX had already issued <u>The Syllabus of Errors</u> in 1869, in which he condemned Modernism, liberalism, and declared that never will the Roman Church ever be allowed to be reconciled with democracy. The Anti-Modernist Oath was a new version of the <u>Syllabus of Errors</u>, about which I knew nothing at the time. Only during Vatican II in 1962 was the Anti-Modernist oath abolished.

However, when John Paul II issued the apostolic letter *Ad Tuendam Fidem* on ecclesiastical discipline, after Vatican II, it provoked dissenters into claiming that the letter was a *second oath* against modernist thought. It was included in the Code of Canon Law to make it more binding. Although John XXIII opened many doors and windows in the church, after his death, his successor, John Paul II quickly closed them. Then, Benedict XVI quickly imposed a regime of intellectual inquisition. What Vatican II had accomplished was quickly forgotten. The anti-intellectual mood of the Roman curia, as well as its lack of charity towards its theologians, was the main reason why I became disaffected of the Roman denomination.

For the course in theology at Saint Benoit-du-Lac, we analyzed every article of the whole Summa Theologiae of St. Thomas Aquinas. It was a real exercise of intellectual rigor. Aquinas combined the whole Christian tradition, which was dependent on St. Augustine with the philosophy of Aristotle. Aquinas used the philosophy of Aristotle instead of that of Plato. With his theory of hylomorphism (body and soul are united in a substantial union), Aristotle made a whole difference. Matter and the body was important, not only the soul, as it was for Plato and Augustine.

While I was at Saint Benoit-du-Lac, I read several manuscripts of Pierre Teihlard de Chardin. He was a Jesuit philosopher, theologian, and paleontologist who contributed to the discovery of the Homo of Pekin, a pre-historic man. Through his scientific explorations he adopted the concept of evolution. Consequently, the Roman Curia would not allow him to publish any of his works during his lifetime because they believed that evolution denies creation. It was their mistake due to ignorance.

Nevertheless, the works of Teihlard were copied by typewriter and distributed throughout French seminaries and Saint-Benoit-du-Lac. The notion of evolution was very important to me because it corrected many of the notions of Thomas Aquinas that denied both evolution of the species and evolution of the individual. It also contradicted the development of the fetus to its full growth as a human person.

One of my problems at Saint Benoit-du-Lac was the lack of opportunity to entertain long philosophical and theological discussions with my peers. We could talk freely only half an hour after lunch and half an hour after dinner. Then, the senior monks led the discussion and young monks, like I, were limited to few casual observations. Dom Hamel, my spiritual director, noticed my depression and suggested that I might have a Benedictine vocation but not necessarily to a strictly cloistered and contemplative style. I needed a papal dispensation to transfer from Saint Benoit-du-Lac to St. Vincent Archabbey, Latrobe, Pennsylvania.

At St. Vincent Archabbey

In March 1956, I transferred to St. Vincent. I had to renew my monastic vows once again. Instead of 100 monks, there were 300. It was a cultural shock to go from French culture and cuisine to German culture and cuisine; from wine to beer. At St. Vincent there was a prep school with 400 students, a liberal arts college with 800, a major seminary with 200, and 50 parishes dependent on the priests of the monastery, dispersed in several states, in Brazil and China. The courses of theology were all taught by monks who had a doctorate in their discipline. Father Demetrius Dumm became my favorite professor. While studying in Rome, he was ordained a priest at Subiaco Abbey; received a Doctorate of Sacred Theology in 1950 from the Pontifical Institute of San`Anselmo. Then, he studied at the Ecole Biblique in Jerusalem and received a Licentiate in Sacred Scripture from the Pontifical Biblical Commission, at the Vatican. His lectures were scholarly and very inspiring. When I was ordained a Roman Catholic priest on May 26, 1957, I invited Father Demetrius to preach at my first public Mass in Montreal.

After ordination, I was assigned to teach theology in our liberal arts college and a moderator in a student dorm. Every weekend, as all other priests of the monastery, I went to different parishes some distance of the monastery, most often 75 miles away, to assist local priests with their duties: hearing confessions two hours on Saturday afternoon, celebrating two Masses and preaching on Sunday morning, and driving back 75 miles to the monastery. What I feared and despised most was during confession, I had to ask the adults if they were married, if they were practicing birth control, and if so, I had to ask them to desist, or else refuse them absolution. This would deprive them from receiving any other sacraments. I thought this was thoroughly immoral. I believed that this attitude of the Church's authorities was unscientific and immoral.

On this day, March 11, 2015, for my daily reading of the Rule of Saint Benedict, I read chapter 33 on "Monastics and Private Ownership: "Above all this evil practice of private ownership must be uprooted and removed from the monastery. We mean that without an order from the abbot, no members may presume to give, receive, or retain anything as their own, nothing at all – not a book, writing tablets, or anything as their own – in short, not a single item, especially since monastics may not have free disposal even of their own bodies and wills."

That is a very strict request. Through the centuries and different living situations, this rule was modified somewhat. Here is an illustration. At Saint Vincent Archabbey, after ordination, I was assigned to teach theology in our liberal arts college and serve as a moderator in a student dorm.

As a student moderator, I was often required to supervise their social activities: chaperon their dances at the country club, share meals with students outside of the monastery in restaurants, going to all kinds of social events. For that purpose we were allowed to keep some pocket money. I found out that many of the monks would go hunting, play golf, go to the opera, and so forth. Having taken tennis lessons when I was young, I volunteered to coach our varsity tennis club. Consequently, I travelled a lot for the intervarsity tennis matches, carried always money in my pocket for eating in restaurants with students. In 1960, my tennis varsity team won the intervarsity championship for Western Pennsylvania. We had two good tennis players: Jim Bender, who had been on the Junior Davis Cup team, and Don Moreno (I am not sure I have the right spelling) who, with his father had won the Men's Double championship in Costa Rica. I was fortunate to win the tournament between the tennis coaches. Eventually I had my own car.

There were also other ways in which the monks of Saint Vincent did not observe strictly the vow of poverty. The director of the Pittsburg Opera, at Heinz Hall, Richard Karp, was a member of the music faculty of Saint Vincent College. He provided discount tickets for the opera in Pittsburgh. Many of the monastic faculty of the college took advantage of that offer. Consequently, I would join several faculty monks to attend each opera. In addition, the owner of the Seven Springs ski resort was a graduate of St Vincent College. He offered discount tickets for the faculty monks who desired to ski.

Jim Stahura, one of my students, who was dyslectic, would come to my office and ask me to read some of his textbooks to him. For Christmas 1960, he gave me a whole ski outfit: skis, poles, boots, ski pants and jacket. I still wear the red sweater he gave me. Jim was very industrious. He made "hogeys" and sold them to other students. He had a business. His father owned a big Christmas tree farm and taught his son how to make money.

I began a faculty monthly newsletter for St Vincent College, entitled <u>Dialogue</u>. It was to encourage the members of the faculty to exchange ideas about the philosophy of education. We had a guest speaker, a great international scholar in the influence of physical education in the context of a holistic education. (Unfortunately, I do not remember his name). We published many good articles on the philosophy of education; unfortunately, after two years I realized that it was no longer a dialogue, but had become a monologue, since too many faculty refused to publish anymore, saying that the college administrators had already decided what philosophy of education they preferred, which left no room for discussion.

I had been influenced by Socrates who said: "An unexamined life is not worth living."

I began reading a lot on the theology of what became known as: "La Nouvelle théologie," a movement in France and Germany that involved a reaction against the neo-scholasticism that then dominated the Catholic schools. It meant going back to the sources, mainly through a scientific study of the Bible, the early church fathers, and using a modern frame of reference. Some of the main authors of this movement were: Yves Congar, Marie-Dominique Chenu, Jean Daniélou, Henri de Lubac, Hans Kueng and Karl Rahner.

Congar was a Dominican theologian who wrote <u>True and False Reform in the Church</u>, in which he remarked that reform always begins from the bottom, from the lay people instead of from above, the hierarchy. Later, Congar was recognized as a leader in the New Theology Movement, and in spite of his condemnation by Pius XII, in his encyclical <u>Humani Generis</u>, in 1950, he was called by Pope XXIII to be a theological authority at Vatican II.

Another of my favorite theologians was Marie-Dominique Chenu. In the early 1950s, he became involved as a friar-preacher in the nascent worker-priest movement and its attempts to evangelize the anti-clerical industrial suburbs of Paris. The new industries had developed outside the residential sections. Some priests, who had been prisoners of war during WWII, became workers in factories instead of waiting in the rectory for the laypeople to come to them. Eventually, in 1953, Chenu was disciplined by Suarez, his superior in the Order of Dominicans, supposedly to save him from worse treatment by the Vatican. Nevertheless, John XXIII called him to Vatican II as a theological expert. He was a forerunner of the back to the sources movement, a return to Scripture and the early Fathers of the Church.

In 1944, Jean Daniélou was named professor of early Christian history at the Institut Catholique of Paris. He produced several historical studies, including <u>The Bible and the Liturgy</u>, which provided a major impetus to the development of the new theology. I read many of his books. He was called by John XXIII as a theological expert at Vatican II.

Karl Rahner, a Jesuit teaching philosophy at Freiburg, delved into the philosophy of Kant, Maréchal, and Heidegger. In 1962, with no prior warning, his superiors told him that he was under Rome's pre-censorship, which meant he could neither publish nor lecture. His outspoken frank approach to faith issues and his creative, challenging stance on theological foundations had gotten him into trouble with the Vatican authorities. Nevertheless, John XXIII appointed him as a theological expert at Vatican II. The basis for Rahner's theology is that all human beings have a latent awareness of God in any experiences of limitation in knowledge or freedom as finite subjects. Because such experience is the condition of possibility for knowledge and freedom as such, Rahner borrowed the language of Kant to describe this experience as ``transcendental.`` In his book, Homanisation(1958), Rahner describes the limits of Catholic theology with respect to evolution. He does not deal simply with the origin of man, but with his existence and his future, issues that can be of some concern to the evolutionary theory. Rahner claims, "the fulfillment of human existence occurs in receiving God's gift of Himself, not only in the beatific vision at the end of time, but present now as seed in grace.``

Hans Kueng studied philosophy and theology at the Pontifical Gregorian University in Rome. His doctoral dissertation was The Doctrine of Karl Barth and a Catholic Reflection, published in 1964. He concluded that the differences between Barth and the Catholic theology of justification did not warrant a division in the Church. The book included a letter from Karl Barth, attesting that he agreed with Kueng's presentation of his theory. I had earlier read his Council and Reunion, in 1960, in which he declared that Rome will not be able to be reconciled with the Reformation until it goes through its own reformation.

In 1960, he became the first Roman Catholic theologian to publicly reject the doctrine of papal infallibility, in his book Infallible? An Inquiry. In the course of his study Kueng examines papal encyclicals and statements, conciliar pronouncements, and the whole concept of the magisterium, and concludes that there is no such thing as an infallible proposition. Using the encyclical Humanae Vitae as his point of reference, Kueng brings to light some of the recognized errors that have been made by the magisterium in the past to demonstrate that certainty of faith is not assured by papal pronouncements, ecumenical councils, or even the Bible, but rather is grounded in the truth of the message of God himself in Jesus Christ. Nevertheless, Pius IX declared that ``the definitions of the Roman pontiff are irreformable of themselves (and not from the consent of the Church.)`` (DS 3074) Such a definition makes the Pope infallible, by himself, without the consent of the Church. Such a definition, Kueng suggests, that the notion of *infallibility* be replaced by that of *indefectibility* – the perpetuity of the whole Church in the truth of God's word despite the possible errors of any of its parts.

Kueng recognizes that "a Petrine ministry in the Church makes sense and every Catholic will affirm it. But the pope exists for the Church and not the Church for the pope. His primacy is not a primacy of ruling, but a primacy of service.``

Jesus told the apostles, who were arguing among themselves about who was the greatest, brought a child before them and said: ``The rulers of this world like to lord it over others; but you shall not do this, you are to be servants, not rulers.`` Jesus offered a power of service not a power of domination .

Consequently, in 1979, Kueng was stripped of his license to teach as a Roman Catholic theologian, but carried on teaching as a tenured professor of ecumenical theology at the University of Tuebingen. He was never excommunicated, and did not abandon the Roman Catholic Church. He wanted to work for its reformation from the inside. He became a theological expert at Vatican II. I read several of his books: On Being A Christian; Christianity and the World Religions: paths of dialogue with Islam, Hinduism, and Buddhism; Judaism: Between Yesterday and Tomorrow; A Global Ethic for a Global Politics and Economics.

In his book on <u>Infallibility, An Inquiry,</u> Kueng mentions that ``According to Vatican II the pope is bound to govern the Church collegially. But the encyclical (<u>Humanae Vitae</u>) was issued in uncollegial solo effort. This is true and the authority of the encyclical is seriously compromised by the fact that The Pope decided against overwhelming majority of specialist theologians, bishops, doctors, demographers, and other experts. They had worked on and discussed the matter for years, and yet he neither took the official report of the commission seriously nor convincingly refuted it. Further, he prevented a discussion and a decision on the question at the council by a peremptory intervention and also, after some initial hesitation avoided a later consultation of the world-episcopate and even of the synod of bishops. Finally, he reached a decision when the church herself was in a state of doubt. As a result of such a procedure, the credibility of the encyclical was seriously placed in question from the very beginning by the Pope himself.``

That is what provoked Garry Wills to write <u>Papal Sin: Structures of Deceit,</u> in which he mentions the historical and doctrinal dishonesties of Paul VI . That is what provoked also the rejection of papal authority by the most famous English theologian, Charles Davis, who wrote <u>A Question of Conscience,</u> to explain his reasons for leaving the Roman denomination.

Lately, I read his memoirs in two volumes: <u>My Struggle for Freedom</u>, and <u>Disputed Truths.</u> In the first of these books, Kueng painted a moving picture of his personal convictions, including his relentless struggle for a Christianity characterized not by the domination of an ecclesiastical inquisition group, but by Jesus. In <u>Disputed Truth</u>, Kueng ends with the removal of his accreditation as a Catholic teacher after more than a decade of measures against him by the authorities. In striking parallel to this, runs the career of a fellow Tuebingen professor, Joseph Ratzinger, who by the end of the book has risen through the Catholic hierarchy on a course which will eventually lead to his election as Pope Benedict XVI. I considered this pope as a "Grand Inquisitor" due to his silencing of 110 Catholic theologians and biblical scholars. In 1965, I heard Kueng speak on *Intellectual Freedom in The Church,* at Yale University; in 1966, I heard him speak on the same subject at the Institut Catholique, in Paris. I agreed with his views that the Roman Curia was the greatest enemy of diversity in the Roman denomination.

On Being a Christian (1984), by Hans Kueng, is a work of exhaustive scholarship, born of the author's passionate belief in Jesus Christ as the center of existence. He assesses the impact of other world religions, humanism, science, technology, and political revolutions. He sifts through the theological controversies within the Christian community itself and affirms the vitality and uniqueness of Christianity by tracing it back to its roots. Kueng examines what it means to be a Christian today: the role of Christian ethics in a social and political context, the relationship between Christians and Jews, the organization of a community of believers, and practical suggestions for dealing with personal crises of faith.

In 1991, Kueng wrote Global Responsibility: In Search of a New World Ethic. I quote the good review of Lonnie Turnispeed:
"The thesis of this book is described succinctly in the opening words of the Introduction:

No survival without a world ethic.

No world peace without peace between religions.

No peace between or ethical guidance from the religions without dialogue between religions.

Turnispeed adds: "No sustainable world ethic apart from religion and no dialogue without a strong commitment to truth."

A new world order is emerging and it does not need a unitary religion and a unitary ideology, but it does need some norms, values, ideals, and goals to bring it together and to be binding on it. Kueng argues that "the basic ethical principle must be that human beings may never be made mere means. They must remain an ultimate end, and always a goal and a criterion." For him, only religion can provide the basis on which human beings can take actions often required in specific instances which are in no way to their advantage, which in no way serve their happiness or any communication, but rather can require of them an action against their interests, a "sacrifice which in an extreme case can even call for the sacrifice of their life."

Kueng recognizes, however, the difficulties of turning to religion as a basis for a global ethic. Religions must acknowledge that today we cannot get "fixed" moral solutions from heaven or from a holy book. Rather, the solutions have to be worked out by human beings using all the resources given them. Seldom are there situations so clear that there are not also moral reasons for an opposite decision. Despite their very different systems of dogmas and symbols, religions do have several ethical perspectives in common. These can provide a foundation for moving toward a global ethic."

In 1993, Kueng drafted A Declaration Toward a Global Ethic, in cooperation with the Council for a Parliament of the World's Religions staff and trustees. He identifies the Golden Rule: "What you wish done to yourself, do to others!" The four essential affirmations as shared principles essential to a global ethic are:

1. commitment to a culture of non-violence and respect for life;
2. commitment to a culture of solidarity and a just economic order;
3. commitment to a culture of tolerance and a life of truthfulness;

4. commitment to a culture of equal rights and partnership between men and women.

This declaration was signed at the Parliament of the World's Religions gathering in 1993 by more than 200 leaders from 40+ different faith traditions and spiritual communities. Since 1993 it has been signed by thousands more leaders and individuals around the world. As such, it established a common ground for people of faith to agree and to cooperate for the good of all. Kueng became my most influential author.

Another theologian who inspired me was Matthew Fox. He was a Dominican priest, educated at the Institut Catholique of Paris, mainly by Chenu. When he came back to this country he taught at a Roman Catholic college in Chicago. In 1976, he started the *Institute of Culture and Creation Spirituality,* which developed an alternative pedagogy that diverged from orthodox Catholic theology and would eventually lead to severe conflict with church authorities. The institute's programs integrated the visceral, emotional and intellectual connections that Fox asserted early church mystics had had with their faith.

In 1983, Fox moved the *Institute of Culture and Creation Spirituality* to Oakland, California. Cardinal Joseph Ratzinger began a series of inquisitorial attacks on Fox. Among Fox's most controversial teachings was a belief in "original blessing" which became the title of one of his most popular books. The concept was in direct contravention of the Roman Catholic doctrine that people are born into original sin.

In his book, <u>Original Blessing</u>, Fox contrasted two spiritualities: one centered on Fall-Redemption spirituality, and the other focused on Creation-Centered spirituality.

The original spirituality begins with the creation story, which was the original blessing. Its spokespersons were: the Yahwist author, the wisdom writers, the prophets, Jesus, Paul, Benedict, Francis, Aquinas, Hildegarde, Eckhart, Cusa, Teilhard, Chenu. It begins with God's creative energy, cosmic, emphasizes extrovert meditation, ecological thinking, welcoming of body and soul, focused on humility as friend of one's earthiness, hopeful, universalist, cosmic Christ.

In contrast, the Fall-Redemption spirituality begins much later with the concept of original sin developed first by Augustine, Thomas a Kempis, Bossuet, and Cotton Mather. Faith means "thinking with assent." It is patriarchal, ascetic, views death as the wages of sin, and holiness as a quest for perfection; expects a return to a state of perfection and innocence.

In 1993, Cardinal Ratzinger ordered the expulsion of Fox from the Dominican Order, and imposed on him a year of silence. During that year, Fox visited the various Christian communities in South America that were influenced by Liberation Theology. There he recorded the various assassinations of Christian missionaries by soldiers trained at the School for the Americas, in Georgia. When he came back to the USA, he was received as a good priest in the Episcopal Church by Bishop Swing of San Francisco. I would visit him after my sessions with the Jesus Seminar.

I read Matthew Fox's book, <u>The Pope's War: Why Ratzinger's secret crusade has imperiled the Church and how it can be saved.</u> Fox wrote about eight of the 110 theologians that Ratzinger silenced and denounced. He then mentions Ratzinger's allies: Opus Dei, the Legion of Christ, and Communion and Liberation – three groups that Ratzinger protected while attacking theologians and spiritual movements that did not fit his criteria of super right-wing politics and religiosity. How can the Roman Denomination subsist with such fifth column that undermines its mission?

In my teaching, I used many ideas borrowed from ``La Nouvelle Théologie,``and from Teihlard de Chardin. In 1959, I was elected chairman of the Catholic Theologians for the area of Pittsburgh. In that capacity, I organized the first ecumenical theological conversations between Catholic, Protestant, and Orthodox theologians, all with the ecclesiastical approval. When Vatican II was announced, I was asked by the Bishop of Pittsburgh and my Archabbot to desist from meeting with the Protestants. I was told that we had to wait till the Roman Curia would tell us how to speak with Protestants. I was a regular contributor of book reviews for the Journal of Ecumenical Studies.

In 1960, I wrote a chapter of the book, The World of Teilhard de Chardin, edited by my friend Robert Francoeur. The title of that chapter was *"The Dynamics of Cosmic Love according to Pierre Teihlard de Chardin."* I had the permission of my Archabbot to publish that. Later on, he had forgotten, when he reproached me for having written this article, after the apostolic delegate to Washington had written to all bishops and religious superiors to prevent their priests from writing or saying anything in public in favor of Teihlhard de Chardin.

In 1960, I wrote a dissertation entitled: <u>The Search of God according to Saint Benedict,</u> in fulfillment of the requirements for a Master's degree in Religious Studies. I mentioned that Saint Benedict did not seem to find God in Rome, where he had been sent by his father to study. At that time, there was a civil war in Rome, in addition to a dispute between two wealthy families hoping their son would become the bishop of Rome. Instead of pursuing his studies in Rome, Benedict decided to retire to a monastic life to pursue his search for God. I lent this thesis to a friend who never returned it.

In 1960, I was invited by the dean of the Department of Religious Studies at the Catholic University of Washington to write a book on <u>The Sacraments of Christian Initiation</u>. I researched how the sacraments of baptism, confirmation, and Holy Eucharist were celebrated in the early Christian centuries. I found out that baptism was celebrated normally by the local priest, or even by any baptized Christian, in case of emergency. The sacrament of confirmation was normally administered by the local priest at the same time as the baptism.

In an early Christian document, we read that the candidate for baptism was usually divested of his secular clothing, immersed completely in water for his baptism, then, vested with a white garment, then anointed by the priest for confirmation and invited to receive his first Communion. That was the normal way for Christian Initiation. It was only in the fourth century that the administration of Confirmation was reserved to the bishop, in Latin Christianity. The reason for this reservation, according to Saint Jerome, was to give honor to the bishop as the leader of the diocese. Until that time, the local parish priest confirmed, as it is still the custom in the Orthodox Church and in missions of the Catholic Church.

As for the Holy Eucharist, it was not until the thirteenth century that the theological explanation for the Real Presence of Christ in the sacrament borrowed from the philosophy of Aristotle the distinction between substance and accidents. Thus, at the consecration, the substance of the bread and wine was transubstantiated into the body and blood of Jesus, while the accidents of the bread and wine (their sense perceived appearance) remained as before. However, according to Aristotelian philosophy, there is a transcendental relation between a substance and its accidents; no separation can be conceived. Thus, the theory of transubstantiation is a rationalistic explanation for a mystery, which is nonsense according to Aristotelian philosophy. In contrast, Luther preferred to speak of consubstantiation: the physical presence of bread and wine as well as the spiritual presence of the body and blood of Christ. Calvin spoke of the real presence in terms of the faith the believer. The Swiss reformer, Swingli, spoke simply of a memorial. The council of Trent spoke of the Real Presence as the object of faith, which could be explained in terms of the theory of transubstantiation. I preferred to keep the mystery of the Real Presence without the philosophical explanation. Consequently, my religious superior refused to grant me the Nihil Obstat (the ecclesiastical permission) for the publication of the book that had already been accepted by the Dean of the Religious Department of the Catholic University. I think that book was valuable; unfortunately, it was never published.

In my course on Christian ethics, I mentioned the inspiring social encyclicals of the Roman Pontiffs: Leo XIII, Pius XI, and Pius XII. When they spoke of providing to all workers the minimum wage to support their families, I wanted to find out if that was true with the secular workers on the campus. I suggested to my students to find out. When I mentioned what I had done at a faculty meeting I was called a "Lutheran" for daring to question the policies of the administration. I found out that it is politically incorrect to question what authorities have done.

In 1960, I was elected as the most popular teacher at Saint Vincent College. At that time, we had five African students on scholarship, eager to learn about human rights and racial justice; but no Black Americans. The Africans were unable to be served in restaurants in Latrobe. The editors of the student newspaper decided to make a survey of the situation. They interviewed the mayor, the chief of police, and the chairman of the chamber of commerce. These all denied any racial problems in Latrobe. Although there were six mini-steel factories in Latrobe, none hired any Blacks. The only work the Blacks could do was to wash the floors of restaurants at night and live in a ghetto. The student editors published their findings.

Of course, the newspaper was distributed not only on campus, but in the town of Latrobe. The businessmen of Latrobe came on campus to require from the administration of the college the retraction of the statements of the editors that was damaging to the reputation of Latrobe. The editors refused; the administration suppressed the newspaper. A radio station had been installed on campus without the appointment of a faculty advisor. The Free Voice of St. Vincent went on the air and published the events. 800 students went on strike for a week. National media was on campus. I was asked to address the student body. I spoke on freedom of conscience according to Pius XII, and freedom of the press, according to Karl Rahner.

My Archabbot called me on carpet. He said: ``You were born to be a heretic. We do not want you to teach theology any more. But, we need someone to teach medieval philosophy." Once again, I was accused of being politically incorrect. I had studied thoroughly the neoscholastic philosophy, but I was now a modern philosopher, pragmatic and empirical. Fortunately, my superior offered me the opportunity of getting a doctorate. So, I agreed to attend the Pontifical Institute of Medieval Studies, at the University of Toronto, in Canada.

In September 1962, I began my studies at the Pontifical Institute of Medieval Studies with courses in medieval history, history of philosophy, history of theology, history of canon law, history of medieval art and architecture, paleography, and medieval Latin. Something that surprised me was during a breakfast with Etienne Gilson, one of the most important medieval scholars in the modern world, I mentioned my admiration for Pierre Teihlard de Chardin. He responded: "But, he is a heretic!" I was surprised that such a medieval scholar ignored what had developed since the middle ages, and was ignorant of modern science.

While studying at the Medieval Institute, I took courses from Father Gregory Baum, a

Canadian theologian who was advising the Canadian bishops at Vatican II. He would fly back and forth between Toronto and Rome, bringing us the first, second, and the third drafts of the councilor documents. Thus, I could witness the various theological positions at Vatican II.

Every Friday, we had high tea at the Institute, according to the English custom. For this opportunity, we invited the faculty and students of St. Michael`s College, which was next door to the Institute. It was at one of these high teas that I met Joan. She told me that she would often usher for the artistic performances of the University of Toronto, and received in return some complimentary tickets. She invited me to accompany her to one of these concerts. She told me that she was thinking of becoming a Benedictine nun, and that since I was the only Benedictine monk on campus, she would like me to be her spiritual advisor. She would come every morning to be my acolyte at the daily Mass and recite with me the Daily Office. She grew up in Lakewood, a western suburb of Cleveland in an American Baptist family. When she went to Smith College in Massachusetts, she abandoned the practice of religion and registered as a pre-med student. In her junior year, however, she met a Roman Catholic law student at the Harvard Newman Club, along with many other R.C. intellectuals, and became herself a Roman Catholic.

She was torn between her relationship with the R.C. law student and the thought of becoming a Benedictine nun. She had made several retreats at Regina Laudis, a French Benedictine monastery in Bethlehem, Connecticut. In April 1963, she made her reservation for a retreat at Regina Laudis. Mother Abbess told her they were without a chaplain for that month. With Mother Abbess's agreement, Joan offered me to become chaplain to the nuns while she was making her retreat. For the summer, my only responsibility was to work on a medieval manuscript, written in medieval Latin, of the commentary of Thomas Aquinas on the metaphysics of Aristotle. I could do this anywhere; so I went to Regina Laudis. On Wednesday, Mother Abbess asked me for an interview on Joan's potential to become a nun. I told her that as far as I knew Joan had been a Roman Catholic only for a few years and she was still thinking as a Protestant. For instance, when I told her what the Pope had said recently, she responded: "That's his personal opinion." Mother Abbess agreed with me that Joan needed to experience a lot more the Catholic ordinary way of life, and take another two years before trying again her vocation. Joan returned to Boston, where she worked in surgery at the Children's hospital. She had trained as a technical assistant at Johns Hopkins Hospital the previous two summers. I returned to Toronto to work on the medieval manuscript.

Encounter with the Episcopal Church

In August 1963, I attended the World Anglican Congress in Toronto. There, I heard the Archbishop Michael Ramsey of Canterbury speak; later, a woman from Africa spoke. When a motion came on the floor, they had equal voice and equal vote. In contrast, at Vatican II, more than 2,000 men, priests, theologians, and bishops were invited with voice and vote; only 12 women from across the world were invited with no voice and no vote. When the opening service of Holy Communion was offered, all the men were able to receive communion within the communion rails; the women had to wait after the service was over to receive communion in a side chapel. To my mind, this was a sort of mini-excommunication. It confirmed in my mind the continuing oppressive policies of the Roman Church.

I had already read the history of the Anglican Communion, many books by Anglican scholars and agreed with them, more than with some of the Roman authorities. I sought an interview with the Episcopal Bishop of Massachusetts and asked him to accept me in his diocese. I wrote to my Archabbot Rembert Weakland, telling him that for peace of conscience I would prefer to become an Episcopalian. He wrote back telling me that I was making the grievous sin of apostasy, but if I ever repented, I would be considered as a prodigal son and received back in the monastic community. I never thought that I was leaving the Catholic Church, but only the Roman denomination.

My mother had given me a chalice when I was ordained a priest. When I left the Roman church the monks of St. Vincent asked me to return the chalice to the monastery, saying that to use it in an Anglican service of Holy Communion would be a profanation. I thought this was totally un-ecumenical to deny the validity of sacraments outside the Roman Catholic denomination. I phoned my mother and asked her opinion. She responded that she would be perfectly pleased to receive communion from me when she would attend one of my celebration of Holy Communion. I refused the intemperate request of the monks and kept my chalice which I use every time I celebrate Eucharist in the Episcopalian service.

After the final examinations at the Pontifical Institute of Medieval Studies I invited my sister Thérese and my brother Paul-Emile to visit me in Toronto. We all went together to Stratford, Ontario, to the Shakespeare Festival theater to attend three of the Bard's plays. Then we drove to Montreal, a nine hour trip. During those long hours I revealed to Therese and Paul-Emile my decision to leave the Roman Catholic Church and to become an Episcopalian. They were shocked and asked for my reasons. Then we argued what had once been my belief and what was still theirs: "outside of the Roman Catholic Church there is no salvation."

Now I believed in Jesus Christ as my core belief, and that the Roman denomination was not the only one faithful to the Gospel. The Roman

Church was un-ecumenical in leaving the Anglican Church out of the apostolic tradition. History can demonstrate that the Roman Church became very sectarian at the Council of Trent. When we arrived in Montreal the whole family was gathered in Mother's apartment, all looking very sad. I froze on the threshold. Mother came forward and kissed me, and said: "You do not have to explain anything; I understand you." I had written her several letters to explain what I was doing. That satisfied her. The only one who did not agree was my oldest sister, Sister Marie-Rose de la Trinité. Until her death she maintained that I would not be saved unless I went back to the monastery. She exhibited the intransigence of the Roman mentality.

One moral problem I had for many years in the monastery was the habit of masturbation, which I regularly confessed. It was the chard in my flesh which I did not seem to overcome. The book of Marc Oraison, La Question Sexuelle, - gave me some comfort. He was born in 1914, became a physician from the medical school of Bordeaux, in 1942, and served in WW II as a medical doctor. He studied theology at the Institut Catholique of Paris, was ordained priest in 1948, obtained a doctorate in theology in 1951. He wrote some twenty books on psychology and individual morality. He considered masturbation a natural development of male sexuality and approved of contraception, when there are good moral reasons.

He claimed the encyclical of Paul VI, Humane Vitae, was not an act of papal infallibility, but rather a proof that papal infallibility is a heresy. I had read that encyclical and determined that it confused the notion of natural physical law with that of natural moral law, as understood by St Thomas Aquinas. To intervene between the sperm and the ovum is against the natural physical law, but not against the natural moral law, which according to Aquinas, is an act of our moral conscience and therefore free. If a woman decides for good reasons of health or economics to prevent conception, she is morally free to do so, without sinning. In 1930, the Anglican bishops wrote a letter in which they approved the pill for contraception for moral reasons. On 1931, The Pope responded with an encyclical in which he condemned all forms of contraception. Father Charles Curren, an outstanding
moral theologian at the Catholic University of America in Washington, D.C. taught that

contraception was morally acceptable when there are sufficient reasons to prevent an unwanted pregnancy. For this reason, he was forced from his tenured position at the Catholic University, and is now teaching at the Southwestern Methodist University, in Texas. Moreover, the invention of the contraceptive pill in 1960 was due to a good Roman Catholic physician at Harvard, Dr. John Rock.

Recently, I read Benedict in the World: Portraits of Monastic Oblates, edited by Linda Kulzer and Roberta Bondi. In chapter 5, on ``Faith in Action: The Lives of Patrick and Patricia Crowley,`` by Margaret Colleton, I found out that the Crowleys had been summoned by Pope Paul VI to participate in the fourth meeting of the Papal Birth Control Commission. They were driving force of the Christian Family Movement initiated in 1943. That was why the Pope chose them.
Of 58 members, there was a small minority, women and married couples were included. The majority found compelling arguments to reform the Church's ban on contraception which did not have a defensible foundation in Scripture, history, reason or science.

Garry Wills wrote in <u>Papal Sin: Structures of Deceit</u>: "As soon as people began to think independently about the matter, the whole structure of deceit crumbled at a touch. The past position could not be sustained, even among these people picked by the Vatican itself, much less among Catholics not as committed as these were. And it was absurd to speak of the non-Catholic world as ever recognizing this "natural law of natural reason." By the end of the fourth session, opponents of change had become a very small minority. During the last session Patty gave a candid and moving presentation. In the years since the rhythm method had been approved, couples using it as a form of birth control had discovered that it had some serious flaws. I always considered the rhythm method was a kind of Russian roulette.

With the help of Notre Dame sociology professor and fellow commissioner Donald Barrett, the Crowleys had conducted a survey to analyze these concerns in detail. They sent questionnaires to CFM couples throughout the world and received three thousand replies from eighteen countries. While some couples did find it an effective method   of birth control, most were dissatisfied with it for two reasons. Because most women do not have regular menstrual cycles, the method did not prevent pregnancies as successfully in practice as it should have in theory. In addition, couples found that it placed undue strain on their marriages by requiring them to abstain from intercourse during the time when their bodies led them to desire it most strongly. "

In the end, 15 voting members of the commission decided by a margin of 9 to 3 (with 3 abstentions) that the Church's teaching could and should be changed. Wills reports: "Cardinal Ottaviani and Father Ford, seeing how things were going, had prepared a document of their own." They secretly lobbied to discredit the commission's report and to "reconvert" the pope, who had been impressed upon first reading it. They were successful" Paul disregarded his own delegation's conclusions and issued Humane Vitae in 1968. Like hundreds of theologians, the Crowleys publicly dissented. They were disillusioned .

I had read also some books on St Augustine's conception of sexual morality. Before his conversion of Christianity, Augustine was once a Manichaeist, which involved the belief in two ultimate realities, a god of good, responsible for our soul, and a god of evil, responsible for our body. His conversion to Platonism reinforced that conception. His conversion to Christianity did not totally eliminate that conviction. He had a troubled youth. He began to live with a woman who was not of his social class. That relationship could not be legalized because of Roman laws prohibiting marriage between social classes. From this union he had a son, called Deodatus (given by God) with whom he entertained some philosophical dialogues. Yet, he never once mentioned the name of that woman with whom he lived faithfully for nineteen years in a common law union.

His mother, Monica, forced him to abandon that woman and introduced him to a woman of his own social class, whom Augustine did not like. After this, he had a series of immoral sexual encounters. When he became a bishop he wanted only celibate priests in his diocese because he felt that the sexual act, even between a married couple, is always sinful by nature, although it can be forgiven by the blessing of marriage. This was why he conceived the notion of original sin which existed neither in Judaism, nor in early Christianity, nor in Eastern

Christianity, nor in any other religion. That is why he decided that children need to be baptized, forgetting that baptism is primarily an incorporation into the mystical body of Christ, making us members of his Church. In his autobiography, Augustine mentions his sexual attraction to the breast of his mother as evidence of original sin. What a horrible view of human nature created by God!

The practice of priestly celibacy was greatly influenced by St Augustine, who required that all priests in his diocese be celibate. At the Council of Nicea, in 325, one bishop proposed the celibacy of the priesthood, but it did not get a second.

It is important to know that the Council of Nicea (325) was convoked and presided over by the Emperor Constantine. He invited all the bishops to his summer home, while he was still the Presiding Pontiff of the pagan Roman religion, before his baptism. He suggested the term "homoousios" to signify the divinity of the Son of God, Jesus, equal to the Father. It is interesting to know that as the Roman Emperor, he was considered divine and the Son of God. It was only on his death bed that he was baptized.

Until the eleventh century, marriage of priests, bishops and popes was normal. Because of the decline of morality during the Dark Ages, the practice of priestly celibacy was suggested as a form of moral reformation in the Western Catholic Church. Laws were passed to impose clerical celibacy. It declared priestly marriage illegal, but not invalid. It was considered a common law marriage. Consequently, priests, bishops and popes continued to marry. But they had to pay a tax on their "concubine" until Luther discovered that hypocrisy. The Council of Trent made clerical marriage not only illegal but invalid. And so it has been since then.

Now, there are some Ecumenical Catholics who believe that clerical marriage is morally acceptable; they even accept priesthood for women. There is such an ecumenical community that meets at St. Paul Episcopal Church, in Fort Collins, every Saturday afternoon, and one in Longmont meeting at a Presbyterian church every Saturday afternoon. I attended one of their meetings. So, when I left the Roman Catholic Church, I thought it would be morally acceptable for me to marry.

In September 1963, I moved to Cambridge and found employment as a research librarian in Harvard Lamont Library. I phoned Joan, as the only person I knew in the Boston area, and told her about my becoming an Episcopalian. If she were attached to the Roman Catholic Church, I would say: "Adieu." Otherwise, if she wanted to become an Episcopalian with me, I would resume our friendly relationship. She agreed and we were both received in the Episcopal Church by Bishop Anselm Phelps-Stokes. A month later, we were married in the Church of the Advent, in Boston. Joan continued to work at Children's hospital and I continued to work at Harvard Lamont Library. We both applied for admission to the graduate schools of religion at Harvard and Yale.

Harvard wanted me to work with Heiko Oberman, a Lutheran medieval scholar. After 16 years of living in a medieval institution, I preferred to go to Yale to work with George Lindbeck, a Lutheran scholar, who had been the official delegate at Vatican II for the Lutheran Church of America. He was teaching a course on Vatican II and a course on contemporary Roman Catholic theology. That was the area in which I wanted to concentrate. Joan worked on the Greek New Testament and early Christian theology. For my doctoral dissertation, I wanted a subject that would force me to go to France, where I had never been. Sydney Ahlstrom, one of my advisors, had just returned from a sabbatical in France. He told me that the archives of Maurice Blondel were now opened to scholarly research. I had never read anything of Blondel, since he was considered a heretic in the Roman Catholic Church.

The French Modernist Crisis was caused by a priest, Alfred Loisy, who refuted Adolph Harnack`s book, <u>The Essence of Christianity.</u> Harnack reduced the core of Christianity to the revelation of the Fatherhood of God and the brotherhood of all men. The rest, he wrote, was a pure corruption of the Gospel by the Roman Church. Loisy had already adopted the scientific method for the study of Scripture, first developed by German Protestant scholars. He wrote <u>The Gospel and the Church</u>, in which he demonstrated that Harnack had based his theory on a passage of ecclesiastical tradition, a passage from St. Matthew, not on Scripture alone, which was the Protestant approach.

On the other hand, Loisy suggested that the contemporary Church does not teach exactly the original Christian gospel, but the result of a long evolution of doctrine. Henry Newman had written a book on <u>The Development of Doctrine.</u> For instance, the doctrine of seven sacraments directly instituted by Christ was an exaggeration. Loisy said; "Penance and marriage were not considered as sacraments until the middle ages." <u>The Gospel and the Church</u> was put on the <u>Index of forbidden books</u> and Loisy was excommunicated. I found that on his tomb the single word "Priest" identified him. From his writings, he revealed himself as a good believer in God and in the human ministry of Jesus, in spite of the many calumnies said about him. Many Roman Catholic scholars who adopted the scientific methods for the study of Scripture were also condemned.

I found out that Blondel was at the center of the Roman Catholic Modernist crisis in France. So, I read everything I could find on him at Yale and in American university libraries. After two years at Yale, we planned to go to France. We had then a five month old baby, Michel Benoit. He was baptized at Christ Episcopal Church at Yale, in New Haven, Connecticut. We boarded an Italian liner with 1500 American students going to Europe to study.

I had obtained a grant from the Canadian Council of the Arts for $1500 (I was still a Canadian citizen), and obtained a student loan for another $1500. When we arrived in Paris, I bought a new 1966 Peugeot for $1900.00 (this was equivalent to one million francs). Frenchmen joked that I was a millionaire. We had a letter of introduction from the Bishop of Massachusetts to the Dean of the American Episcopal Cathedral in Paris. This allowed me to become an assistant priest for every Sunday services at the Cathedral, while Joan served as the supervisor of the small children, during the services.

Experience in France

One of the great experiences I had while serving at the Episcopal Cathedral was when the Anglican Archbishop Michael Ramsey was received by the Catholic Bishop of Paris at the Cathedral of Notre Dame, I was asked to substitute for the Dean, who felt sick, as the chaplain for the Archbishop Ramsey. That was quite an emotional experience to be in the great French Roman Catholic Cathedral, now as an Episcopalian priest. After the service, I was driven in the Dean`s chauffeured limousine, in my liturgical cope, to the British Embassy for the reception. When I thought it was time for me to leave, I could not find the limousine. In the meantime, the Dean felt better and called his chauffeur to pick him up to come to the reception. I had no money in my pocket to call a taxi. So I walked the whole length of the Champs Elyzées, in my liturgical cope. Passersby might have thought I was an actor going to a play. The next day, Archbishop Ramsey was given a honorary doctor of theology degree at the Institut Catholique of Paris, and called "The Patriarch of the Catholic Church in England."

We could not afford an apartment in the center of Paris, near the Episcopal Cathedral, limited as we were to the grant of $2800 a year for living expenses from the Kent Fellowship I had received. A good one-room apartment on the second floor of a residence on the river Marne became our home, in Joinville-le-Pont. Toilet was public in the corridor. We had a beautiful balcony overlooking the river. Every day, I would jump behind an autobus to go to the terminal of the subway, and there travel to the center of Paris where I did my work.

I obtained permission to explore the archives of Blondel. Many of his archives were kept at his daughter's apartment on the river Seine in Paris. I went there every day to go through his huge correspondence. Although the apartment was luxurious, it had no central heating. In the winter, I wore my thermal underwear and Elizabeth Flory, Blondel's daughter, brought me a cup of tea. Later on, I drove to Aix-en-Provence, where Blondel had taught the last twenty years of his life. His long time secretary, Nathalie Panis, aged 78, was still living. She shared with me a lot of information of Blondel's life and work. She also guided me through many of the old Greek and Roman remains in Provence. I then went to the library of the Old Louvain University in Belgium, where the majority of Blondel's archives are being kept.

Maurice Blondel (1861-1949) wrote History and Dogma in 1904, at the apogée of the French Modernist Crisis, in an effort to explain how critical scientific methods applied to Scripture can be reconciled with doctrinal formulations. He rejected two incomplete and incompatible solutions, which he labelled *extrincisim* and *historicism*. *Extrincism* represents the extreme tendency to impose dogmatic conclusions on historical science, while *historicism* represents the opposite extreme tendency to reduce dogmatic formulations to what can be ascertained by history alone. These opposite extremes reveal an idealistic illusion which confuses reality with intellectual abstractions. For an intermediary between history and dogma, Blondel pointed to *tradition.* The synthesis is realized neither in the facts alone, nor in the ideas alone, but in *tradition* which embraces the whole life of the Church, the facts of sacred history, the efforts of theological reasoning, and the accumulated experiences of the faithful "under the direction of a divinely assisted pope." Blondel believed that his own philosophy of L`Action (1896), his doctoral thesis, could supply the rational justification for such a conception of *tradition.*

In his efforts to interpret accurately History and Dogma, I consulted the extensive literature, as well as the archives of Blondel, Laberthonniere (a close friend of Blondel), and Loisy. I interpreted this treatise in the context of Blondel`s extensive correspondence, preceding, during, and following its publication. Ever since Blondel wrote the Letter on Apologetics, in 1896, in which he criticized harshly the pseudo-philosophy of the neo-scholastic revival, and proposed a frank acceptance of modern critical philosophy as the right method of approaching the religious problem, he was accused of being an innovator seeking to undermine traditional beliefs, and the father of philosophical modernism.

History and Dogma was written as a personal apology for his own orthodoxy. His spiritual advisors, Wehrlé and Mourret pressed Blondel to write a rebuttal of Loisy. Yet, Blondel sympathized with Loisy's call for the intellectual independence in biblical studies, just as he sought the same intellectual freedom in philosophical issues. From the documents examined in this dissertation, it should be clear that Loisy and Huegel were even less inclined towards historicism than Batiffol and Lagrange, who proclaimed themselves defenders of orthodoxy, and who did expect to prove the supernatural nature of the Gospel and the Church by history alone. Whenever there was a question of a Roman Curia condemnation of Blondel, there was always a bishop or a cardinal who came forth to his defense. As a wealthy landowner, he often invited bishops and cardinals to his home.

Blondel was never condemned during his lifetime, but after his death in1949, four of the books of his student and friend, Henry Dumery, a priest teaching at the Sorbonne , in which he expounded the philosophy of Blondel, were put on the Index of forbidden books. History and Dogma saved Blondel from a condemnation when Pius X issued the syllabus Lamentabili, and then encyclical Pascendi; but it was only in the relaxed atmosphere preceding Vatican II that its influence was really felt through the impact of the "Nouvelle Théologie" which he partly inspired. Until Vatican II, the suspicion of being a modernist created an atmosphere of paranoia in the Roman Catholic Church.

Search for employment

In February 1967, in Paris, I received a letter from the dean of the Episcopal School for Ministry, in Cambridge, Massachusetts, offering me a teaching appointment. The letter did not reach me until five months later. The dean of the school in Cambridge did not have my address in Paris, and sent his letter to Yale, which sent it to me only five months later. I flew immediately to

Boston, only to find that the position had been granted to someone else half an hour earlier, since they assumed I was not interested. Later, I received a letter from the University of California, in Santa Barbara, offering me a teaching position. Joan said that if I wanted to go there, I would have to go alone. She did not want to go west of the Mississippi, nor south of the Mason-Dixon Line. Her intransigent attitude caused me a lot of trouble in the future.

After five months I had completed my thesis and sent it back to Yale to be corrected and approved by my three faculty advisors: George Lindbeck, Sydney Ahlstrom, and Jaroslav Pelikan, The title was: <u>The Significance of Maurice Blondel's Treatise: History and Dogma in the French Roman Catholic Modernist Crisis</u>. It was never published because I had used many originals of Blondel, while his family had granted to the Jesuits the exclusive right of publication. The thesis, however, can be read from the University microfilms. I gave several talks on this subject to scholarly meetings.

We got in the Peugeot, and with Michel, our first son, still in his first year of life, we travelled throughout France, Spain, Italy,

Switzerland, Germany, Holland, and Belgium. We were lucky to use the <u>Fodor Guide</u> for travel in Europe on $5.00 day for each adult:

$2.00 for bed and breakfast,

$2.00 for a seven course dinner;

$1.00 for a bottle of wine, a French baguette, and some cheese for lunch.

We returned to Yale in August 1967, without a job. The dean of the graduate school at Yale told me there was an opening for a substitute for the professor of Humanities at Wilberforce University, in Xenia, Ohio, who had suffered a heart attack. That was a 98% Black university. I enjoyed teaching the history of art, literature, philosophy and religion in the last 20 centuries of Western civilization. Joan, however, did not like it. She was always hoping that I would get an appointment at Smith College, from which she graduated.

I did get an appointment at Wells College, in Aurora, New York, on the Cayuga Lake. It was second best in the mind of Joan. Wells was founded by Henry Wells, the founder of American Express and Wells Fargo. In the chart, it mentions that Wells should be a finishing school for future wives of successive businessmen. As a matter of fact, President Cleveland, as bachelor in the White House, would come in his private railroad car, parked on a side track, and offer parties to the faculty while he was courting a student of Wells, whom he later married.

I was five years at Wells College and enjoyed teaching there the history of Christianity in five semesters, political ethics, and some philosophy. Several times a month I went to Cornell, 25 miles north of our campus, to visit with some professors, the Episcopal and the Roman Catholic chaplains. There, I met Dan Berrigan, the famous Jesuit, anti-Vietnam activist, who entertained an underground church for anti-Vietnam young men who hoped to escape to Canada. He introduced me to Rosemary Ruether, a famous Catholic theologian, who irritated some bishops by her book, The Church against Itself, in which she criticized some politics of the Church. I read also a book written by seven American theologians, from various Christian denominations and from Judaism, w
ho visited Vietnam and described the unethical and immoral actions of the American soldiers. They wrote a report of their findings in A Question of Conscience.

I read also the <u>Pentagon Papers,</u> on which the husband of Rosemary Ruether had worked for the Rand Corporation. It described the deceptive tactics of the USA that got us involved in the civil war of liberation of the Vietnamese. The country had been socialist for 2,000 years until the middle of the 18th century when it became a French colony, and only then was introduced to capitalism. The French lost that colony to the Japanese in WW II. The Americans were then looking for an outlet to its industrial overproduction after the war. Vietnam appeared as a solution for a door into Asia. The American position of opposition to communism was a deception. While the French soldiers preferred to remain in France to reconstruct their country, the Marshall Plan, which was supposed to assist France in its reconstruction was earmarked in part to be used exclusively for the reconquest of a former colony, which the French did not want. When I was still at Saint Benoit-du-Lac, I met a French Benedictine monk who was now an admiral in the French navy, who was on his way to Indochina. France did not allow a dispensation from the military service to the clergy. When many French soldiers deserted the fight in Vietnam and lost the battle for Diem-bien-phu, the Americans picked up the plum, hoping to gain the Asian outlet it was seeking for its industrial overproduction.

I found out that the notion of a "Just war" was due to St. Augustine, who declared that error does not have a right to exist. He recommended that the Roman Emperor Constantine, who was now a Christian, should persecute the heretical Donatists in North Africa. Since then, the Roman Church has pursued heretics, by violence when necessary. So many wars, persecutions, inquisitions and violence were the result of that false notion of "Just War!" In the atomic age, that notion is even more false and meaningless. That is why I became a pacifist.

In the early 70s, a new interest in Black studies motivated several professors to introduce some new courses. I was asked to introduce a course on Black religion. First, I went to Cornel to interview those who were teachings Afro-American studies. I was asked if I had ever attended a Black church, which I had not. So, it was suggested that I attend the Black Aenon Baptist Church in Rochester, New York. When I arrived there, I was impressed by how well dressed were the members of that church in an economically depressed area of Rochester. When the minister saw me as the only white person in the back of the church, he came to introduce himself and invited me to join him on a chair at the front. He invited me to read the gospel, which I did in the formal custom of the Episcopal Church. When I made the first pause, a shout of: "Alleluia," stunned me. This continued whenever I made a pause in the reading. I became accustomed to that interruption. I began to wave, sing and shout as the other members of the congregation did. It was a very moving, emotional, charismatic service with people fainting all over.

Next Sunday, I invited some of my Wells College students to attend the service with me. They were also transformed by the experience. I went to the Rochester School of Divinity, and invited a Black Caucus group of seminarians to come to Wells to conduct a Sunday evening worship service. Normally, the chaplain, a "dead-of-god" theologian, would conduct an intellectual lecture for that service. This time, with the Black Caucus, it was a revival session. My students, sitting in the front row were able to react appropriately, while the remainder of the students sat still frozen in their seats. Only on a second

Sunday, did they all respond sympathetically. We had broken a social barrier. One of the books I used in my course on Black Religion, was that of James Cone, <u>Black Theology and Black Power.</u> He tried to identify liberation at the heart of the Christian gospel and blackness as the primary mode of God`s presence. He wanted to speak on behalf of the voiceless black masses in the name of Jesus whose gospel he believed had been greatly distorted by the preaching and theology of white churches. He found in the great prophets of Israel the voice of liberation from slavery.

Another book that I used in my courses at Wells College was that of Rosemary Ruether, <u>A Liberation Theology, Human hope confronts Christian History and American Power</u>. I remember going to Washington, D.C. for a conference of the American Historical Society when I was invited to the home of Rosemary Ruether and her husband, Herman, who was working for the Rand Corporation. Rosemary led us in a celebration of Holy Communion, in which she presided. She said, in the early Church many women, as the head of a household, did preside over the Eucharist. Later on, that summer, Rosemary was going to L.A. to deliver a lecture on the misogyny of the early Fathers of the

Church. She said ironically she had titled her lecture as "The Penis of Saint Augustine: the misogyny of the early Fathers of the Church." During that week we kept her three children in our home.

Rosemary Ruether also mentioned the various movements of liberation in Latin America, especially the base communities where lay Christians gathered to study the Bible and reflect with that background on their own experience of living under political and social oppression by the wealthy landowners supported by many bishops coming from wealthy families. She mentioned Gustavo Gutierrez and Leonardo Boff. Recently I purchased a book written in 1988 by Harvey Cox, a great Harvard Baptist theologian who described the <u>Silencing of Leonard Boff</u>. He wrote: "The conversion of Constantine and his endorsement of Christianity as the official religion of the Roman Empire was in reality, as Leonardo Boff maintains, a paganization of Christianity, not a Christianization of paganism. It could have been the other way, but instead the church took on the empire's institutions: its laws, its bureaucratic centralization, its ranks and titles. Even the terms used to describe the church's organization –

"diocese" and "parish" – were absorbed directly from the empire." Boff says this set the church on a path of power that continues today and that we must hasten to end." (Leonardo Boff, <u>Church: Charism and Power: Liberation theology and the Institutional Church</u>. p. 51). The power of Jesus used by his disciples, *exousia,* is the power of love. The power of the imperial Rome was *potestas*, the power to lord it over others as the pagans do. In contrast, the disciples were to become like servants, not eager to dominate and rule. Harvey Cox writes: "Boff is sure that the cause of the historical Jesus who was poor, weak, powerless, critical of the social and religious status quo of his time, will shine forth again."(p. 54).

In August 1972, I went to Quebec City with eight of my students from Wells to attend an international conference on Peace in Vietnam. We met scholars, religious and political leaders from around the world, including some Vietnamese from both north and south of the country. Unbeknownst to me, some photographs taken of our group with some communist leaders were submitted for publication in the alumnae magazine of Wells. When the parents of my students saw the pictures of their daughters with some communist leaders, they were upset. So when I came up for tenure, I was told by the president of the college that for reasons of economics I could not get tenure, even though my department and the dean of the college had approved of it.

Joan decided I should go back to Canada, since obviously, in her mind, I did not like the USA. I had noticed that Joan would never come with me when I was serving in local parishes, nor did she ever come with me to the meetings of clergy and spouses. She preferred to meet with the wives of college faculty, where she would speak more with the men than with the women. Our marital relations were over and we got a divorce. She did not see anything wrong with divorce; most of her friends in college were from divorced families. I thought we could work it out, but Joan was determined to be separated. At that time she regarded Nixon as a hero; I thought he was the equivalent of Hitler, especially after his order to bomb Cambodia.

After the divorce, Joan returned to the Catholic Church. I told her that she would never be able to remarry, as a divorced woman. She answered: the Catholic chaplain at Syracuse

University, where she was studying, told her that our marriage was never valid, because I was a priest, even though we were married as both Episcopalians. That did not bother her. She remarried with an atheist. Then, she argued over some moral issues with the bishop of Helena, Montana, where she was living. My pilgrimage to Nepal, Tibet, and Thailand later on might have inspired her to make her own pilgrimage to Tibet, spend time in a Buddhist monastery, and become a Buddhist herself. In my opinion, Joan's understanding of religion was a pragmatic one, depending on the circumstances of life.

We had adopted a second son, Pierre, a year earlier. He was born in Ithaca from an Irish mother, a graduate student at Cornell and a French military who was an exchange student for a month at Cornell. When she founded out she was pregnant, she immediately made arrangements to give up the baby for adoption at the Children and Family services in Ithaca. He was baptized by the Episcopal Chaplain at Cornell University, in Ithaca, New York. He was not a quiet baby like his older brother who was breast-fed; Pierre cried all the time. He was bottle-fed, and that made a big difference in his general attitude. He never felt secure in his early life.

Joan had gone to the University of Syracuse and obtained a Master's degree in library science and artificial intelligence. For her dissertation, she wrote a book as a guide for research in the development of new drugs. This book was sponsored by UNESCO. As a result, she was granted a month in Paris. When she returned she found a good position at Bristol-Meyers, as a consultant for research in the development of new drugs. The rest of her business career was spent in this kind of work. She is now an international consultant for the development of new drugs, traveling to Japan, Germany, and South Africa. She owns three houses in Helena, Montana, and a condo, in Saint George, Utah, where she spends the winter.

Meanwhile, without a job, without a family, without a home, I left my books and clothing in my office at Wells College until September, and with a tent I settled in a State park, near Ithaca. It was difficult for me to find a teaching job at a moment when I was greatly depressed. Fortunately, in the Fall I was invited to substitute for the Rector of Grace Episcopal

Church, in Cortland, New York. The rector had open-heart surgery. I found a congregation divided between those who were "born again" and speaking in tongues and the rest of the church community, most of which were affiliated with the State University of New York, in Cortland. One day, two ladies from the parish came to my house to pray with me so that I might receive the gift of tongues. I said I would rather pray for an increase in the gift of love. When the rector recovered from his medical problem, I was assigned to take care of three small parishes, each 15 to 25 miles apart, but which did not want to join together. I received only a cash salary with housing benefits in Homer, New York. That was only 30 miles south of Syracuse where my two boys were living with their mother. I could thus visit them and bring them home every second weekend.

While living in Homer, I found some part-time teaching of philosophy at Tompkins Community College, and later at the State University at Cortland. With a grant from the National Endowment for Humanities, I introduced the first course on religious studies in this secular institution. A year later, with another grant from the National Endowment for

Humanities, I organized a seminar on the role of women in academic teaching. Several scholars from other universities attended. The dean of Cortland State University mentioned there was a possibility I might obtain a faculty position. With that expectation, I obtained my American citizenship after 20 years living and working in the USA with a green card. It did not benefit me since Governor Nelson Rockefeller decided to put a freeze on faculty appointments for that year.

(There is a period of my life of which I am very ashamed. I rarely mention it, but for the sake of honesty I will risk losing some portion of my self-esteem. Joyce (not her real name), a member of one of the parishes I was serving, was a great singer, had an operatic voice. She was very popular and the center of attention at parties. She began inviting me to dinner at her apartment. We went together to social events and to concerts. Soon, I found out that at parties, she was drinking too much and began speaking loudly, and sometimes offensively. That bothered me very much, so I ceased associating with her.

After a while, her mother called me in the middle of the night to come and help her to restrain her daughter. Living in a luxury apartment, she had been drinking too much and was disturbing the neighbors. One of them, a retired chief of police, was trying to restrain her, emptying several bottles of gin she had hidden in her apartment. He confronted her with the option of going to an alcoholic rehabilitation clinic or being arrested for public disturbance. Joyce chose the clinic. Once she had recovered, I was able to obtain a good paying job for her through some friend of mine, but I did not resume our relationship.

Later, when I had moved to Baltimore and was interim rector of St. Mark`s on the Hill, I found myself very lonely in the big rectory. It became evident to me, talking with other clergy, that a divorced priest is very unlikely to obtain a parish, but if he is re-married, it was then possible. I called Joyce, still living in Homer and asked about her alcoholism; she declared that she had completely overcome it. I invited her to come and visit me in Baltimore. She did and we renewed our friendship. We found a good priest to offer us some good pre-marital counseling. After which, we begged the Bishop of Maryland to allow us to re-marry. The whole parish was very supportive and prepared a splendid wedding.

Joyce found a good job with the civil service administration in Baltimore.

Every Friday we went out for dinner. For the Thanksgiving weekend, I invited my two sons to visit us. I bought four tickets to see "Babes in Toyland." That morning, Joyce refused to come with us, saying she would stay home and prepare a good dinner. When we returned, she was drunk and began swearing at us. I was completely ashamed and realized that TGIF was not a good choice.

Soon, I realized that having wine for dinner was not very good for Joyce. When I was offered the position of Vicar of the Church of Epiphany in Grove City, I thought the move from the big city would eliminate the regular TGIF. Joyce joined the choir and with her beautiful voice was a great addition. However, it soon appeared that Joyce was secretly drinking wine with some medical pills for her headaches. On Christmas Eve, she did not appear in church. When I returned to the rectory, I found her drunk and cursing. Under our bed there was a hammer and a butcher knife. She said she was afraid I might assault her. I left immediately and slept in my office. I refused to return to the rectory until she would promise to receive some joint counseling. That, she refused to do, saying all psychologists were crazy. Eventually, she moved out of the rectory, returned to Baltimore and filed for divorce. Several times, she called me to renew our friendship, which I refused due to the nightmares I had lived through. Never again, will I ever live with an alcoholic.)

In 1978, I was invited to be chaplain to higher education in downtown Baltimore. This position had once been fully subsidized, but then, it offered only half salary with no fringe benefits. Since it was supported by three wealthy downtown Episcopal parishes, there was always hope that someday it would be fully subsidized. I was responsible for pastoral services at the University of Baltimore, the Medical and Law schools of the University of Maryland in Baltimore, the Antioch College of arts, and the Maryland school of music.

With the dean of the medical school, I organized a conference on medical ethics with a grant from the National Endowment for Humanities. To earn more money, I accepted to be the interim rector of St. Mark's on the Hill, in north Baltimore. When the majority of the parish indicated they would like me to be their rector, I had a problem. According to the diocesan rules, an interim cannot be a candidate for rector in the parish he is serving. I was persuaded to resign as interim rector; then, I became a candidate for rector. When the final vote took place, a divorced woman in the congregation made such a fuss over the fact I was divorced that I had to leave.

In 1980, the Bishop of North Pennsylvania offered me an
opening as the Vicar of the Church of Epiphany, in Grove City, Pennsylvania. I had already received an offer to be chaplain at the University of South California, but turned it down because that would take me too far away to see my boys. I phoned Joan in Syracuse to tell her of the offer from Grove City, which would allow me to see the boys at least once a month. In return, Joan told me that she was getting re-married with Heidi Van Duym, the director of the National Endowment for Humanities for the State of Montana, and was moving to Helena, Montana. What a shock! Earlier, she had refused to move west of the Mississippi. While Joan was often traveling from Monday to Friday for her business, Heidi, an atheist, took care of the boys. He

destroyed their religious beliefs. When I met them again, only once a year, they would say: "Dad, quit that bullshit." I was never again able to talk religion or spirituality with my two sons; we were living in two different spiritual worlds.

I went to Grove City where the church had not had a priest for seven years. In the meantime, a self-employed businessman had taken over the office of the priest for his own and served as both the senior warden and treasurer, a double responsibility that is not normally accepted in the Episcopal Church. The bishop wanted to appoint a new treasurer. I asked the senior warden to submit the financial records to have them certified by a notary. It took a whole month before he told me that he had not kept books. He had told the vestry there was a surplus in the checking account; in contrast he gave me a bunch of unpaid bills to the amount of $8,000. The bishop wanted to subpoena him; I told him I would use pastoral methods. That did not work. At first, the parish could pay me only a cash salary, with no life and health insurance and no pension plan. After a year, they were not even able to pay the cash salary. The bishop asked me to resign. I asked him: "What do I do now, I cannot collect unemployment insurance." He said: "You can go back to the monastery." What a pastoral advice! I moved out of the rectory and rented a small house in the woods outside of Slippery Rock and registered at the University for a Master's degree in counseling psychology.

For five months I lived on credit cards. It was during this period that I received a phone call from Michel during the middle of the night, begging me to allow him to take the surname of his stepfather, Heidi Van Duym. I was baffled! I thought if Michel was a girl, it would not matter much is she was to marry. At that moment I was financially unable to continue paying the child support money, since I had no job. Joan was threatening me to use legal means to extract those from me. So I consented to Michel's request. A week later Pierre called me and said: "Father, I will keep your name." That pleased me very much. My own son was no longer called by my name, in contrast to my adopted son.

I have always been addicted to sailing since I was in the Canadian navy during WW II. When I was at Yale, I bought an 11-foot Sean Snark, a fiberglass sailboat, 30 pounds weight which was easy to carry on top of the car. We used it very much in the summer of 1965, when we drove as far as South Carolina for our vacation. We sailed in every body of water we encountered. Later, when I was teaching at Wells, I bought a 14-foot O'Day sailboat; then, a 19-foot triple keel sailboat with a cabin not large enough to stand in, but sufficient for me and my two boys to sleep in. In 1982, I realized that my two boys were now teenagers, taller than I, and we would not be able to fit in the 19-foot boat. I could not afford a bigger boat. I found, however, a catalogue from Luger Boat Kits, which offered a discount of 50% on a manufactured sailboat if you were willing to assemble the kit by yourself. I phoned Mr. Luger in Burnsville , Minnesota, to tell him I was interested in the 27-foot sailboat. He told me if I were serious, he would pay my airfare to fly to Burnsville and see one such sailboat fully assembled by a professional in their showroom.

I accepted the offer and flew to Burnsville, where I was greatly impressed by the sailboat fully assembled, and I put down the down-payment. Mr. Luger took me to a steak house and asked me: ``Did you ever assemble anything like that before?`` I told him I assembled toys for my children, but never anything as big as a sailboat. He said I would receive 35 pages of blueprint to guide me. Then, I flew to Helena, Montana, to visit with my boys. We went skiing together at Bridger Bowl and had a good time.

In the spring of 1982, I drove to Helena to pick up the boys who would be with me for a month. Coming back east, we stopped in Burnsville to pick up the two axle trailer with the fiberglass shell of the 27-foot sailboat sitting on top. Since we were late, the workers of the Luger factory were gone home; only a night watchman was present. He connected the trailer to the hitch of my new Oldsmobile car, but unfortunately he used a hammer to make the connection (something forbidden by those who know). We stayed overnight in a motel. I was hoping to pass by Chicago before the major traffic jams in the morning, but unfortunately, the boys got up late, having watched TV late the night before. When we got on the six-lane one way Dan Ray expressway, by Chicago, we were in the middle lane, going 65 miles an hour.

Suddenly, Michel sitting in the back seat called out: "Dad, you`d better stop; there`s a trail of fire behind us." I looked in the rearview mirror and saw indeed that trail of fire. There was a tractor trailer behind me with flashing lights and blocking our lane. With flashing lights on, I came quickly to a stop, called my boys to get out of the car, got my dog in the back seat, could not find his leash, used my belt for the dog, and we all ran in front of the car. As we turned around we saw the car surrounded by flames; soon the gasoline tank exploded. The boys were crying; I kept cool, remembering that I had insured everything before our departure. $25,000 gone in flames. Fortunately, I had insured everything before leaving Grove City. Thank God! Our lives had been saved. The thought that our lives are fragile became impressed in my conscience. I found out that the vibration of the trailer on the road had caused the trailer to rip itself off the hitch of the car. The trailer lagged behind, but was kept in tow by the safety chains. It did come closer to the car and ruptured the gasoline tank, which caused the gasoline to drip. When I stopped, the fire went into the tank and caused the explosion. The police took us to the station to make the official report, and two women from the Chicago Social Services took us to some store to get shoes for the boys and a leash for the dog. I called a friend in Grove City, Dr. Dubiel, to pick us up at the Pittsburgh airport. There were no direct flight to Pittsburgh; we had to go through Louisville, Kentucky.

The next morning, back home in Grove City, I got on my bicycle and rode to the car dealer. I told him my mishap. He said that I was lucky since another buyer had ordered the same car as mine, but declined to buy it. So, I had a new Oldsmobile. When the insurance money came, we went to Sears and Penney to buy clothing for the boys. I re-ordered the same boat kit, but said I did not want to go through Chicago again. I was told they had storage in Long Island, and that was where I got the new version of the Luger 27, at the end of the summer. Meanwhile, we drove to Montreal to visit the family and I went sailing with one of my cousins.

It took me two years to assemble the sailboat. I had to buy some power tools, a step and extension ladders, rubber gloves to work with fiberglass, and ruined many work pants before I finished. I kept that sailboat for 15 years, sailing in many lakes and rivers, and even on the Atlantic Ocean. When I was fortunate enough, I sold the 27-foot sailboat to a veteran and carpenter and bought a manufactured 26-foot McGregor sailboat, which I kept until 2002 after I had moved to Colorado. The boys were no longer interested in sailing with me.

Recently I read the book of Wallace J. Nichols, Blue Mind: The Surprising Science that shows how being near, in, on or under water can make you happier, healthier, more connected, and better at what you do. That explains my fascination with sailing. He wrote: "In a boat, you feel as if you are the master of your fate, captain of your soul." My sailboats were always called: "Oasis."

In January 1982, I was offered to become assistant rector of Fox Chapel Episcopal Church, a northeast suburb of Pittsburgh. I was given a three bedroom house to live in and a full salary, plus fringe benefits for the first time in my priestly ministry. I enjoyed everything at that time. The choir was excellent and we had a first class organist. The liturgy was beautiful. One of my responsibilities was to take care of the teenagers. I would meet with them every Sunday evening for a good program. At one time, I took eight teenagers to go on my sailboat on a lake 50 miles north of Pittsburgh. There was a nice wind when we got there; so we sailed north on the lake. As we were coming back south, the wind died down; I was about to start the motor when the kids asked me to put down the anchor and allow them to go swimming. I knew that the State Park regulations did not allow swimming from a sailboat, but only from a lifeguard protected beach. I saw no one around, so I agreed. The eight teenagers, plus an adult parent, went swimming with a lot of noise, diving from the boat. As they were done swimming I was about to pull up the anchor when a speed boat arrived with two park rangers who told me to stop. They reminded me of the State Park regulations and gave me a summons to appear in court. They said it would cost me $500 for each person swimming. I was devastated. The teenagers said: ``Don`t worry, Father; we will make a bake sale and bail you out of jail.'' I went to court with a lawyer friend of mine who pleaded our case. It cost me $75 for court fees.

Another of my responsibilities was to visit a nursing home. At that place I met a young woman in her early forties, who had ruined her life with drugs and alcohol. I tried in vain to minister to her, but she would curse me. She died while I was away, but the nurses who tried also to bring her to her senses were greeted with blasphemies. She died unrepentant. I spent some time counseling with those nurses.

When a regular parishioner asked me to visit her husband dying in the hospital, I was greeted with this question: "Who are you?" I said I was the assistant rector of the parish where his wife attended regularly, and I came at her request. He said he did not ask for me and told me to leave immediately. He was the CEO of a large steel company, and was accustomed to boss people around.

We had many unmarried people in the parish: single, never married, separated, divorced, widow or widower. I invited all these people, not only from our parish, but from every Christian parish in the area. Within a year we had a list of 80 persons, from age 20 to 80. One of these, the widow of the CEO of a large company, asked me to escort her to the concerts at Heinz Hall. Before the concert, I was invited to the special dinner, in the dining room of Heinz Hall. Every Friday evening we had a social gathering: either wine and cheese, or we would go to a play, a movie, or a dance. One of those Fridays, when Susan found out I was not married, she became very friendly and invited me to dinner at her town house. She did that several times.

Married Life with Susan

Susan had been married 30 years with her first husband with whom she attended the University of Delaware. She graduated with a Bachelor degree in Home economics; he graduated as a petroleum engineer. He began working for Gulf Oil Company where his father was also working. From the bottom of the corporation ladder, in 30 years he moved to the top to be Vice President of that company. When Gulf Oil was absorbed by Chevron, he became the Vice President of that company. They had three children: David, a physician, married with two children, in Houston, Texas; a daughter, Ann, married to the water engineer in Tyler, Texas; a second son, Richard, a lawyer in San Francisco, married with two children. They had lived 12 years in Europe where her husband was in charge of the Gulf enterprises: in Denmark, in Italy, and then, in London, England. When he came back to Pittsburgh, he bought a big house in Pittsburgh, fell in love with the realtor who sold him that house, and came back to London where his wife was still living and asked her for a divorce. After the divorce, Susan went in counseling for two years, until I met her.

With Susan, we went sailing once a week during the summer and engaged in pre-marital counseling with an Episcopal priest, who was also a professional psychologist. Susan became an Episcopalian for my sake. After a year, we petitioned the Bishop of Pittsburgh for the permission to marry, since we had both divorced from our previous marriage. The Bishop said that he allowed lay people to re-marry after a divorce, but not the clergy, for it gives a bad example to laypeople struggling in a difficult marriage. No Episcopal priest and no Episcopal parish from the diocese could allow us to marry. Susan grew up as a Presbyterian. We found a Presbyterian minister, the Pastor of the biggest Gothic church in East Pittsburgh, a memorial to the banker R.K. Mellon. It was a big marriage, with 100 guests, including six Episcopal priests who were forbidden from giving us a public blessing. For our honeymoon, we went to Fairfield Harbour, in New Bern, North Carolina, where I had a timesharing place. We went sailing every day. When we came home, Susan said: "From now on, you go sailing by yourself; I don`t like it." She was an indoor person, with no interest in outdoor activities. In contrast, I was playing a lot of tennis, sailing alone in the summer and skiing alone in winter.

Because of our marriage, the bishop put me under a pastoral suspension (not a canonical one) for a period of three years. I resigned my position at Fox Chapel Episcopal Church. Fortunately, I had just completed an M.A. in counseling psychology at Slippery Rock University. For my senior thesis, I was to do a psychological evaluation of a teenager. A friend of mine (whose name escapes me at the moment), a D.O., offered me his daughter for my work. He told me to call him after my graduation and he would give me work. While he cared for the medical problems of his patients, he sent them to me if they had some psychological problem. That gave me an income of $75 an hour of counseling, he charged to insurance companies through his medical billing.

In 1989, I was invited to become a clinical psychologist at Huntington State Hospital, a hospital for the mentally ill, in Huntington, West Virginia. There I would do the initial psychological evaluations of patients at their admission. The position did not pay very much. Consequently, I sought some teaching position. I found a full-time teaching position of psychology at Ashland Community College, a branch of the University of Kentucky. We were attending

Trinity Episcopal Church in Huntington when the rector asked me to become his assistant. I told him I was under a pastoral suspension from the Bishop of Pittsburgh. He called the bishop and obtained my clearance. When he went on a sabbatical, I was placed in charge of the parish. Fortunately, there was a full-time deacon who covered for me when I was either at the State Hospital or teaching in Ashland. Eventually, I gave up my hospital assignment and focused on teaching psychology, philosophy and world religions (Hinduism, Buddhism, Judaism, Christianity, and Islam), at Ashland.

We moved to a beautiful condo on the shores of Ohio River, in South Point, Ohio. I would cross one bridge to go to Huntington, where I was serving at Trinity Church and sometimes teaching philosophy at Marshall University. The Rector gave his resignation during his sabbatical and the Bishop of West Virginia appointed me as interim rector. I stayed in that position for two years until they found a new rector. I would cross another bridge to go to Ashland. I had a sailboat and kept it at a private dock 75 feet below our condo. From our dining room we could observe the river traffic.

With Susan, I had a wonderful life, although she soon became disaffected from the Episcopal Church, especially the Holy Eucharist which she did not like. She preferred going back to the Presbyterian Church to hear some good sermons. We attended a lot of artistic performances, going to Cincinnati Opera House. In the summer, on the waterfront of Huntington, there was a barge on which a jazz band played the music of all the great popular orchestras, and allowed dancing on the dock. We enjoyed those dances. I went sailing alone or with friends, either on the Ohio River, or at Cave Run Lake, 25 miles away in Kentucky.

In 1990, I had a radical prostatectomy, which left me impotent and incontinent. The prostate, the lymph nodes and the testicles were cancerous. That affected our sex life, and we eventually slept in different bed rooms. The prostatectomy had killed the sex drive, which affected our marriage. Although I tried all kinds of medical means: pills, medical contraptions, nothing worked.

In 1994, I experienced a strange phenomenon. While driving my car, I felt nauseated and dizzy. I stopped by the wayside and waited for an hour until I had vomited and felt better. Later, while teaching psychology, in particular at that time the section on sensation, I felt a surplus of sensation. I sat down, then lay on the floor, while 25 nursing students came to feel my pulse and my heart and finally called 911. I was taken by ambulance to the hospital and spent three days undergoing all kinds of neurological tests. They found nothing, and concluded that I had the *Meniere's syndrome.* Later, to eliminate the dizziness, the surgeon pierced the Mastoid bone and decompressed the left inner ear. From then on, I had no more dizziness, but I lost 90% of hearing in my left ear and 50% in the right ear. That has affected the rest of my life. I had a series of hearing aids, the new ones supposedly better than the earlier ones, with more volume but deficient in quality; hearing aids provided a lot of noise but not the ability to recognize words.

With Susan, we travelled twice to the British Isles on an Anglican pilgrimage; one year, we visited the north of England and Scotland; the next year, we visited the south of England and Ireland. The two pilgrimages were a great boast to our spirituality. In 1992, my son Michel invited me to officiate at his wedding in Boulder, Colorado. I planned his wedding at St. John's

Episcopal Church, in Boulder, but Michel insisted to be married outside, a mile up from Boulder on an esplanade overlooking the city. That was my first visit to Colorado. I fell in love with the Rocky Mountains, and vowed to retire there some day. I gave to Michel and Carrie a honeymoon of two weeks in the Italian Alps, from my ownership of two time sharing places. In 1994, we went to Costa Rica for the wedding of my second son, Pierre. He was marrying Darcie, a girl he had met at a party of his fraternity at the University of Washington, in Seattle. Her father had retired from IBM and with his wife moved to Costa Rica in a wealthy residence. They insisted that the wedding should be celebrated at the Episcopal Church in San Jose, Costa Rica. I officiated at the wedding and we spent two weeks visiting the countryside.

In 1996, I had a sabbatical for six months and spent the time doing some research in many academic libraries: at Yale, Harvard, Institut Catholique, in Paris, the new Louvain library in Belgium, Oxford, Cambridge, and Edinburgh, in Scotland.

I came across a book of Jean Vanier, Becoming Human. Jean Vanier was the son of

The Governor General of Canada, Georges Vanier and Pauline Vanier. My mother was friend with Pauline Vanier, when she and her husband were members of the Church of Sacred Heart, in Ottawa. Jean was born in Geneva, while his father was on diplomatic service in Switzerland. In his youth, Vanier received a broad education in English and French, first in Canada, and then in England and France. He spent much of WW 2 at an English naval academy, preparing for a career as a naval officer. Visiting Paris where his father was Canadian Ambassador, he visited survivors of Nazi concentration camps. Seeing victims, their faces twisted with fear and anguish, he was profoundly moved. He resigned the navy and went to the *Institut Catholique* in Paris, where he obtained a PH.D in philosophy, then taught at St . Michael's College, in Toronto.

Through his friendship with Father Thomas Philippe, he became aware of the plight of people institutionalized with developmental disabilities. He established a community for people with disabilities to live and with those who cared for them. He established such homes in different countries of the world, especially L'Arche, near Toronto, Canada. I thought several times of going to visit him there, but never did. In his book,

<u>Becoming Human</u>, Vanier shares his profoundly human vision for creating a common good that radically changes our communities, our relationships, and ourselves.

One of the man whom he inspired was Henri Nouwen, whose book, <u>Discernment,</u> I am reading now. Henri Nouwen was born in Holland in 1932. Very early he felt a call to the priesthood. After his ordination he went to study psychology as the Catholic University of Nijmegen. In 1964 he went to study at the Menninger Clinic in the USA. Then, he went to teach a Notre Dame, Harvard, and Yale. For several months he lived at the Trappist monastery of Genesee. In the early 80s he lived with the poor in Peru. In 1985 he was called to join L'Arche in Trosly France. Later, he was appointed chaplain at L'Arche Daybreak near Toronto, Canada.

In his book, <u>Discernment,</u> Nouwen mentions that God is always speaking to us – individually and as the people of God – at different times and in many ways: through dreams and visions, prophets and messengers, scripture and tradition, experience and reason, and events. That discernment is the spiritual practice that accesses and seeks to understand what God is trying to say. The books we read, the nature we enjoy, the people we meet, and the events we experience contain within themselves signs of God's presence and guidance day by day.

While teaching religious studies at Ashland Community College, I got involved in the Westar Institute, a scholarly meeting of biblical scholars focusing on the life and works of Jesus. I became a fellow of the Jesus seminar for several years, enjoyed their rational discussion, but missed the absence of faith. The Institute had been started by Robert Funk in 1985, grouping some 150 critical scholars who used a combination of primary sources, secondary sources, and archeological evidence. They published in 1993, The Five Gospels. It included the four canonicals plus the Gospel of Thomas, and listed seven bases for the modern critical scholarship of Jesus:

1. Distinguishing between the historical Jesus and the stories that the gospels tell about him;
2. Distinguishing between the Synoptic gospels and that of John;
3. Identifying Mark as the first gospel;

4. Identifying the hypothetical Q document, found in Matthew and Luke, but not in Mark;
5. Questioning the eschatological (apocalyptic) Jesus;
6. Distinguishing between oral and print cultures;
7. Distinguishing the historical elements in the gospels from its embellishments.

I travelled to Santa Rosa, California once a year in the summer for the seminar meetings. Some of the books I read then were:

Borg, Marcus: Meeting Jesus Again for the First Time;

Crossan, John Dominic: Jesus: A Revolutionary Biography;

Funk, Robert and al.: The Parables of Jesus;

Funk, Robert and al.: The Five Gospels: What did Jesus Really Say

Funk, Robert and al.: The Acts of Jesus: What Jesus Really Do

Miller, Robert: The Jesus Seminar and Its Critics

Borg, Marcus & N.T. Wright: The Meaning of Jesus: two Visions.

According to the Jesus Seminar, Jesus of Nazareth was born during the reign of Herod the Great; his mother's name was Mary, and he had a human father whose name may not have been Joseph; Jesus was born in Nazareth, not in Bethlehem; Jesus was an itinerant sage who shared meals with social outcasts; he practiced faith healing without the use of ancient medicine or magic; he did not walk on water, feed the multitude with loaves and fishes, change water into wine or raise Lazarus from the dead; he was arrested in Jerusalem and crucified by the Romans; he was executed as a public nuisance, not for claiming to be the Son of God; the empty tomb is a fiction; belief in the resurrection is based on the visionary experiences of Paul, Peter, and Mary Magdalene.

Of course, the Jesus Seminar came under criticism regarding its methods, assumptions, and conclusions from a wide array of scholars. Some of their books I read were:

Luke Timothy Johnson: <u>Jesus: The Misguided Quest for the Historical Jesus</u>;

Marcus Borg and N.T. Wright: <u>The Meaning of Jesus: Two Visions</u>.

When I first read Luke Johnson`s book, I was offended by his negative and sarcastic comments on the scholarship of the Westar Institute. Later, when I met him at a clergy conference for the diocese of Colorado, and read his commentary on the gospels, I came to appreciate much more Luke Johnson, a former Benedictine monk, who was equally qualified in critical scholarship, with the added benefits of studying Jesus with the eyes of faith.

Of course, the authors of the New Testament were not direct witnesses of what Jesus did and said. They were members of religious communities, in different geographical areas, writing what had become the traditional faith in their respective communities. Consequently, they were not like modern historians who collect evidence and facts and derive from them certain theories; rather, they were faithful believers who wrote what their respective communities believed. Thus, the canonical gospels are testimonies of faith.

The names of Matthew, Mark, Luke and John do not appear in the earliest manuscripts; these names were given later on, at the beginning of the second century. Mark was first written around 70 AD, forty years after the death of Jesus. Mathew and Luke were written around 85 AD, and John around 95 AD. Without faith, one cannot understand what the authors were saying. Not all the scholars of the Westar Institute were deprived of faith, and consequently, many like Marcus Borg, John Dominic Crossan, and Bishop Spong maintained their faith, although they express it in modern scholarly fashion.

Marcus Borg was born in the Lutheran Church, but abandoned the practice of religion in his college years, because of his scientific studies. Later on, he recovered his faith, which he documents in his book: <u>Meeting Jesus Again for the First Time (1994)</u>. He married Marianne, an Episcopal priest and canon of Trinity Episcopal Church in Portland, Oregon. He is the Hundere Distinguished Professor of Religion and Culture at Oregon State University. Some of his many books are: <u>Reading the Bible Again for the First</u>

Time; The God We Never Knew; The Heart of Christianity; The Meaning of Jesus: Two Visions (1999) written with N.T. Wright; Speaking Christian (2011); Jesus: Uncovering the Life, Teachings and Relevance of a Religious Revolutionary (2006). His work had been translated into eleven languages.

His latest book is titled: Convictions: How I Learned What Matters Most (2014), in which he developed his most bedrock convictions and why they matter. I agree entirely with what Borg expresses as his personal faith. God is best understood in terms of pan-en-theism: God is in everything and everything is in God, without God being identified with the world, which is pantheism. He rejects orthodox theism: God as the Supreme Being, beyond the world, who intervenes occasionally in the world, as in miracles. Borg considers this notion as leading to atheism. Faith is real, even though it is a mystery. Salvation is more about this life than an afterlife. Jesus prayed that the kingdom of God be realized in this world. Jesus is the norm of the Bible. He opposes the historical-factual interpretation of the Bible favored by fundamentalists with a historical-metaphorical interpretation. Many stories in the Bible are prophecies made historical; metaphorical not factual. The substitution theory, conceived in the 11th century by St. Anselm is a distortion of the original historical interpretation that Jesus died because of our sins. This makes God look like an angry father who seeks complete revenge. Such a theory is based on the German code of law in the Middle Ages. Rather, Jesus died because of the opposition of the Jewish religious leaders in accord with the Roman authorities. Along with the great prophets: Amos, Hosea, Isaiah and Jeremiah, Borg views the Bible as a political reproach against social injustice. Consequently, God is more passionate about justice and the poor than about social conformity with the establishment. Christians are called to peace and nonviolence; therefore pacifism is a Christian duty.

In his book, The Heart of Christianity, Borg describes the emerging paradigm of the Christian Tradition as historical, metaphorical and sacramental. The Bible is the historical product of two ancient communities, ancient Israel and the early Christian movement. The Bible was written for the ancient communities that produced it and must be interpreted in their ancient historical context. It is not so very much concerned with the historical factuality of the Bible's stories, but much more with their meanings. The Bible has a sacramental ability to mediate the sacred. Instead of being a divine product with divine authority, the Bible is a human response to God. Instead of being interpreted in a literal-factual sense, it has a historical and metaphorical meaning. Instead of emphasizing an afterlife and the belief in Christ to be saved, it emphasizes a transformation of our life in this world through a relationship with God.

John Dominic Crossan was born in Ireland in 1934 and educated at Maynooth College, from which he received his Doctorate of Divinity in 1959. He did his post-doctoral research at the Pontifical Biblical Institute in Rome from 1959 to 1961, and at the Ecole Biblique in Jerusalem from 1965 to 1967. He was ordained priest from 1957 to 1969. He joined DePaul University, Chicago, in 1969 and remained there until 1995. He is now a Professor Emeritus in its Department of Religious Studies. He was co-chair of the Jesus Seminar from 1985 to 1996. He was elected President of the Society of Biblical Literature for 2011-2012. He has written 27 books on the historical Jesus, the Apostle Paul, and earliest Christianity and his works have been translated into 13 languages. Some of his books are: The Historical Jesus: The Life of a Mediterranean Jewish Peasant (1991); The Birth of Christianity: Discovering What Happened in the Years immediately after the execution of Jesus (1998); In Search of Paul: How Jesus's Apostle Paul Opposed Rome's Empire with God's Kingdom. His next book, How to Read the Bible and Still Be A Christian, is to be published in 2015.

In his book, Who Killed Jesus? Exposing the Roots of Anti-Semitism in the Gospel Story of the Death of Jesus (1996) Crossan develops several theses: 1. The followers of Jesus carried Jesus` message to the Gentiles; 2. The Gospels are "prophesy historicized" rather than "history remembered."` 3. The Gospels place the blame for Jesus` death on the Jews and exonerates the Romans, among which the early Christians were spreading.

Bishop John Shelby Spong was the Episcopal Bishop of Newark for 24 years before his retirement in 2001. He is a teaching bishop who makes contemporary theology accessible to the ordinary layperson. He is considered the champion of an inclusive faith by many, both inside and outside the Christian church. In one of his recent books, <u>The Signs of Scripture: Exposing the Bible's Texts of Hate to Discover the God of Love</u> (2001), he seeks to introduce readers to a proper way to engage the holy books of the Judeo-Christian tradition. He considers himself as believer who knows and loves the Bible deeply, but also recognizes that parts of it have been used to undergird prejudices and to mask violence. One of his most controversial books was<u>: Why Christianity must change or it will die (1999)</u>. Spong begins his book by exposing the Apostles creed line by line, then he methodically moves on through the heart of Christian belief, carefully exposing the inadequacies of Christianity as detailed in the Bible and in the traditions of the Church.

I enjoyed the intellectual stimulation at the Santa Rosa seminars, but I needed some emotional relief from that experience by going to spend some time at the University of Creation Spirituality, founded by Father Matthew Fox, in Oakland, California. The Jesus seminar was totally rational; it had no room for faith.

I used that information in the various parishes in Huntington, West Virginia, where I served as the interim rector: 2 years at Trinity;

one year at St. Peter`s Church in Huntington; and six years at St. Andrew`s, in Barboursville, a suburb of Huntington. Unfortunately, these congregations were often influenced by some very conservative members who resisted learning anything new.

In my course on World Religions at Ashland Community College, I used the textbook of Huston Smith, Religions of the World. Smith was born in China to Methodist missionaries and spent his first 17 years there. Upon coming to the USA for education he studied at Central Methodist University and the University of Chicago. He taught at the University of Denver from 1944 to 1947; then at Washington University in St. Louis, Missouri from 1958 to 1973. He then moved to Syracuse University, where he was Thomas J. Watson Professor of Religion and Distinguished Adjunct Professor of Philosophy until his retirement in 1983. During his career, Smith not only studied, but practiced Vedanta Hinduism, Zen Buddhism, and Sufi Islam for more than ten years each. He did not want to study world religions only from the exterior scholarly fashion, but from the interior. He was particularly interested in the mystic traditions of all world religions. In his introduction he claims we cannot know any of these religions from the outside. All we can do is to listen carefully and with full attention to each voice in turn as it addresses the divine. His criteria for inclusion and analysis of religions are "relevance to the modern mind" and "universality". His interest in each religion is more concerned with its principles than its context.

Three important authors I read then were: Rudolf Otto, The Idea of the Holy; Mircea Eliade, The Sacred and the Profane; and William James, The Principles of Psychology, and Varieties of Religious Experience.

In 1998, while I was at Ashland Community College, my librarian friend introduced me to the book of Ken Wilber, The Marriage of Sense and Soul: Integrating Science and Religion. This book provided an answer to my long intellectual and religious evolution. Earlier in my philosophical odyssey, the philosophy and theology of Aristotle and Thomas Aquinas had satisfied me, until I came across the writings of Pierre Teilhard de Chardin. His scientific research and discovery of one of the first humanoid, the Homo of Pekin, convinced me of the evolution of the universe. Since I discovered the books of Ken Wilber, this new development of my intellectual life has transformed my integral vision of the universe.

Ken Wilber is one of the most widely read and influential American philosophers of our time. His writings have been translated into over twenty foreign languages. He lives in Boulder and Denver, Colorado. He has founded *the Integral Institute,* which is now situated near the Denver International Airport, to accommodate the thousands of international scholars who gather there periodically, in order to coordinate their scientific theories. For instance, there are sections for Integral Psychology, Integral Sociology, Integral Business, Integral Politics, Integral Spirituality, and so forth. There is an amazing website in his name, where you can take courses in many of these subjects.

Some of Wilber's books I read include: No Boundary; Sex, Ecology, and Spirituality; Up from Eden; The Spectrum of Consciousness (when he was 23 years old); and a Brief History of Everything. At first hearing , the title of this last named book seems bombastic. But, if you know that he is one of the most comprehensive thinkers of our time, you can verify that he is a rational and humble person. He wakes up at 3am, exercises and meditates for three hours; then reads and writes for ten or twelve hours a day. The <u>Brief History of Everything</u> is an introductory sampler, designed to acquaint newcomers with his work. It contains brief passages from his most popular books, ranging over a variety of topics, including levels of consciousness, mystical experience, meditation practice, death, the perennial philosophy, and Wilber's integral approach to reality, including matter, body, mind, and spirit. I have adopted Wilber's integral vision of four quadrants to summarize my integral vision. The four quadrants include matter, body, mind, spirit, and they allow me to integrate physics, chemistry, biology, psychology, philosophy, theology, and mysticism. The four quadrants include:

1.The upper-left: the mind, interior, individual, intentional; Self, consciousness; psychological sciences, religion, mysticism;

2.The upper-right: the brain, exterior, individual, behavioral; the organism; physical sciences, physics, biology, chemistry;

3. The lower-left: collective, interior; culture and worldview; social studies;
4. The lower-right: collective, exterior, social; social systems and the environment; study of systems, of institutions and social organizations

Buddhist Pilgrimages with Shambhala

In 1999, with Susan, we went on a pilgrimage sponsored by the Shambhala publications for scholars of world religions to Israel and Jordan. We visited all the religious sites. Susan, a conservative Christian, would enter only the Christian sites. At the Jerusalem Mosque, she stayed outside to guard our shoes. We had each day a meditation led by some of the various religious leaders and a lecture on the various World religions. Susan would listen only to the Christian scholars. Before going to Israel I had read some twenty books written by Palestinian authors and wished to meet and interview some of them. I was told I would be arrested if I did so. I found out that Israel is really not a democracy, except for the Israelis, but a concentration camp for the Palestinians. The Wall, built on Palestinian land, prevents the Palestinians to reach freely their farms and other essential facilities. There are 516 checkpoints and roadblocks. The Zionists who dominate the politics in Israel have abused many human rights of the Palestinians. They were condemned repeatedly by the United Nations, but unfortunately the USA vetoed these condemnations, more concerned with its oil interests than with the human rights of the Palestinians. I am a strong supporter of Sabeel, which is an ecumenical grassroots liberation theology movement among Palestinian Christians, other Christians, Jews and Moslems. At one time I wrote letters to the editor of the Huntington newspaper accusing the Zionists of betraying the Torah by their abuses. A friend of mine, a CEO of a big West Virginia company, called me to his office and informed me that the Israeli secret police dealt seriously with those they deemed their enemy. He opened his desk drawer and showed me a big magnum revolver to make his point. We used to meet at his home, invited by his wife for French speaking people.

After the incident at his office, I never showed up at those conversations.

When a similar pilgrimage was sponsored by the Shambala publications, in April 2001 to visit Nepal, Tibet, and Thailand, Susan did not come. We first flew from Los Angeles, through Seoul, South Korea, then to Bangkok, Thailand, and to Kathmandu, in Nepal. In Nepal we visited the Great Stupa of Boudhanath, one of the largest and most significant stupas in the world. From there we walked to the nearby Sechen Tennuyi Dargyeling Buddhist monastery, the most thriving Tibetan Buddhist monastery in the world. I met there a French Buddhist monk, Matthieu Ricard, who lives there. He left a scientific career as a molecular biologist in France to study Buddhism in the Himalayas more than forty years ago. He's been the French interpreter for His Holiness the Dalai Lama since 1989. Matthieu donates the proceeds from his work and much of his time to thirty humanitarian projects in Asia. He gave us a lecture on the Sacred Arts and Iconography of Tibetan Buddhism. Then, we visited Pharping, a small traditional town and popular pilgrimage site for both Buddhists and Hindus.

On April 14, we flew to Tibet, on *The China Southwest Airlines*, flying over five of the world`s highest mountains in Tibet. We arrived at Gongkar airport, at 11,500 feet altitude. We took a bus to Yumbu Lagang, where we visited a Buddhist monastery situated at 12,100 feet altitude. From the top we looked on the valley which had been the route the Dalai Lama, with 80,000 Tibetan monks, took in their flight from the Chinese to Nepal in 1959.

On April 16, we left for Lhasa, where we visited the Jokhang monastery, which dates back to the 7th century. We witnessed the monks chanting their prayers, ringing bells, and blowing their long hollow horns. That evening we were given a lecture on Vayrayana Practice. The next day, we drove to the Tsurphu Monastery, established in 1185. There we heard a lecture on the Five Buddha Family Mandala: Elemental Wisdom. There we witnessed the Buddhist wedding of two members of our traveling group, Abby Higgins and Richard Steward. It was very moving. On April 19 we visited the Potala Palace in Lhasa, which had been the Dalai Lama`s winter palace. It dates back to the 8th century. Then, we visited the Sera Monastery where 300 monks live. We witnessed a traditional debate, a lively event in which monks debate questions surrounding the Buddhist doctrine. We saw hand and body movements, an integral part of the debate ritual. It night have been an exercise to rehearse the memory of the principal teachings of Buddhism. Later, we attended a lecture of Judy Lief on: "Tiger, Lion, Garda Dragon: The Teachings of the Shambhala." `In the evening we had dinner at the Crazy Yak Restaurant, where the faculty and staff made some final remarks. Then, we were entertained by musicians, dancers, and actors from Tibet. They wore very colorful costumes. The day before, we had been taken by bus to a monastery at 15,000 feet. The next day, I hired a Toyota Land cruiser, a Chinese driver and a Chinese guide to go to a mountain pass, at 16,000 feet. I was eager to go as high as possible.

On April 21, we flew to Bangkok, Thailand. After breakfast, a boat ride on the Chao Praya river took us to Ayuthaya, the former royal capital of Siam, where 33 kings of various Siamese dynasties reigned until the Burmese conquered it. I went shopping with a guide and bought a traditional formal dress for Susan, which she never wore. On April 23, we flew to Chiang Mai, in the north of Thailand. It was established in 1296, in a fertile valley at 1,000 feet, and shrouded by mountains. We enjoyed a tour of the Wat Phra Tat Doi Sutep, with its guilded temple and commanding view of the countryside. On April 24, we drove to the elephant farm, where we watched the elephants bathe in the river and do some work and tricks. I had an elephant ride. We returned to Bangkok and transferred to the international airport terminal for the return flight to the USA.

In May 17-20, 2001, I participated in a Sufi conference at the YMCA camp in Blue Ridge, North Carolina. Sufism is the mystical tradition within Islam. The opening talks on Sufism were given by Andrew Harvey and Llewellyn Vaughan Lee. Lee spoke first with a calm and contemplative attitude. He said: "We are here to share our love for God, for the sake of love, for what is real; we are to give birth to something, by offering ourselves.`` In contrast, Harvey spoke in a very dynamic and fiery voice, like a Hebrew prophet. He is an ecumenical Christian mystic who studied at Oxford and wrote many books on mysticism, some of which are: The Direct Path; The Son of Man; The Essential Mystics; The Return of the Mother, and so forth.

Living in Colorado

One of the main reasons why I wanted to move to Colorado was the fact that my two boys were living there: Michel in Boulder and Pierre in Denver. All their teenage years I could afford to see them only once a year, during their summer vacation. I wanted to renew some conversation, especially concerning their loss of faith.

After eight years of my suggesting to Susan that we should retire in Colorado, she finally accepted to come and stay 10 days in a motel in Loveland, to search for a convenient place where to move. This was Thanksgiving vacation. We searched in Boulder (where I would have preferred to live, because of its liberal atmosphere), in Longmont, Fort Collins, and Loveland. Finally we found a suitable place in Loveland and signed a conditional contract that we would first sell our condo, in South Point, Ohio. I thought we would sell our condo within a few months. While Susan went back to our condo in South Point, I rented a small apartment in Berthoud, in order to go skiing. For the past eight years, I had spent a week each winter with Michel, in Boulder, to go skiing during my winter semester break. In the middle of January 2002, Susan phoned me to say she had decided not to move anymore. She had moved every 3 or 4 years during the 30 years of marriage to her first husband. She asked me to sell her my half ownership of the condo, and to buy myself a house in the mountains of Colorado. She did come to visit me the next year, on her way to visit her son in California, but still decided not to move.

In February 2002, I bought a small 3-bedroom house on the corner of South Estrella Avenue and 15th street SW. For income, I applied at all the four universities in the neighborhood: Colorado State University, in Fort Collins; North Colorado University, in Greely; Colorado University in Boulder; and Regis University in Denver, without success. I did teach psychology for a summer session at the local Aims community college.

A priest friend of mine offered me a six-week-old yellow Labrador retriever, I called Tammy. I enjoyed her very much, took her to a park every morning to train her by throwing a tennis ball that she retrieved. I took her also to a training school; unfortunately, the only thing she learned was to retrieve a tennis ball. If I released her from her dog run, she would run away; I could not retrieve her unless I showed her a tennis ball. One morning, before going to St Paul Episcopal Church as a substitute for the Morning Eucharist, I stopped at a dog run to let Tammy get some exercise. After I called her back and put a leash on her, she jerked and I fell face down on pebbles. When I arrived at St. Paul, Joyce Wooley, a member of the altar guild was appalled at seeing my bloody face. After nursing me she offered to train my dog. After two years of lack of success I wish to give away Tammy. Joyce mentioned that her son, Eric, was looking for a dog. I gave him everything, kennel, food, and documents. He still has her.

At first I attended All Saints Episcopal Church, in Loveland, but found the congregation to be too much inward looking and conservative. I did go to St. Luke`s Episcopal church In Fort Collins, which had a very good choir and organist. I was asked to give some lectures to the adult education program on the findings of the Jesus Seminar. The Rector found these too liberal for his congregation. I then attended Plymouth Church of Christ in Fort Collins where the pastor had studied with Marcus Borg. I enjoyed his sermons, in one of which he mentioned that there were only two churches in Fort Collins that were liberal on social issues and biblical studies:

Plymouth Church of Christ and St. Paul`s Episcopal Church. With this information I switched to St. Paul and found it very agreeable to my biblical and theological views. Father Bill Bacon was about to retire. I stayed there during the period of two interim rectors, and enjoyed very much the lively liturgy and adult education program.

One of the interim rectors was Bob Davidson, the son of Bishop Davidson. He married early at 19 with Linda, who was 18. They were both lay ministers in Kentucky, supported by the Presbyterian Church. They had three children: Kyle, Mimi, and Bethany. Kyle is social worker in Seattle. Mimi went to Yale DivinitySchool and graduated with a M.Div. and married her classmate, Nick.

But after three years, I realized that every Sunday, I was driving past All Saints, three miles north where I lived, for another 12 miles to St. Paul, in Fort Collins. I resigned myself to stop and stay at All Saints.

Father Sathi Bunyan suggested my name as the interim rector of the Church of Holy Comforter, in Broomsville. My first Sunday there, on the eve of the war in Iraq, I had read how the Pope, the Roman Catholic, the Episcopal and the Methodist bishops had all condemned this war begun on lies and false premises. Thus, I preached a sermon against that war. After the service, three men accosted me, declaring they were veterans of the Korean War and disapproved of my sermon. They said they would leave the parish if I were to become the interim rector. The senior warden told me that these three men were the wealthiest members of the parish, and if they were to leave, the parish would be in financial straits. He tore up my contract and I left. At All Saints, I was met with the disapproval of my pacifist views by several members. Nevertheless, I had the support of the retired bishop Bill Davidson, who was a leading member of the Episcopal Peace Fellowship. Every Saturday morning we would demonstrate, with some Mennonite and Methodist members, with peace signs at the intersection of Eisenhower and Taft. I was never asked to preach at All Saints, although I did so whenever I was invited to substitute in other parishes.

Father Sathi Bunyan was a very generous man: he gave to all who came to him for help; he supported many charitable organizations like the shelter for the homeless and the store where furniture and clothing could be purchased at a discount. He was very good at visiting the sick, either at home or in the hospital. But he did not like controversies and so he provided a comfortable pew for those who prefer peace. When he retired after 29 years of being rector of All Saints, I hoped we would get a priest with more socially liberal views, eager to challenge us to confront critical issues. We did get a young priest-in-charge, Father Travis Smith, with a recent Master's degree in Divinity, who had a more laissez-faire attitude towards children running loudly around the church. This bothered me and the older members of the congregation. After two years, the vestry chose to explore a different approach to the ministry. They invited Father Spencer Carr to be the interim rector. With his large experience of both the business world and a late vocation to the priesthood, Father Carr provided a very good transition from a well-loved rector and opened us to the possibility of new visions for the parish life. He challenged us to open our minds to new and unexpected outcomes.

The final choice was for our first woman Rector. Nina Churchman was educated as civil engineer, married also an engineer, had two children, a daughter who graduated in environmental studies and who works in Denver, and a son, who graduated from the University of California, and is beginning his professional career. Some 15 years ago, Nina discovered a priestly vocation, went to Yale Divinity School and was ordained an Episcopal priest. Her husband has recently died of cancer. She served several parishes and finally was a hospital chaplain in Denver, before her election as Rector of All Saints.

This was a refreshing change. I was glad to greet a former Yale graduate, and we shared many theological views in common. Nina has breathed new spiritual life in the congregation and challenged parishioners to think in new ways. In particular, every Sunday, we view and discuss the video "Living the Questions." Every Tuesday and Wednesday morning we have 20 minutes of silent meditation. Every Wednesday evening we discuss Richard Rohr's book, <u>Things Hidden: Scripture and Spirituality</u>, or see a video like: "What the Bleep is it all about? "

In 2003, I volunteered at McKee Hospital, at The Hospice Center, and for the homeless shelter in Loveland. There I met Edie Brown, a retired widow, who volunteers for all kinds of charitable services. We became good friends, attended some concerts together, and even made a retreat at St. Walburga. She is good Christian from a nondenominational church, uninterested in the liturgy, which for me is very important. She does not understand the notion and importance of sacraments. She has two sisters: Maryann, living in Cheyenne, Wyoming, and Cynthia married to Don, a retired welder, living in Loveland.

Two of my good friends at Wexford are Don and Lucille Hendricks. Don is a liberal Roman Catholic, retired professor of biochemistry, while his wife, Lucille, is a nondenominational Christian, a mystic and liberal thinker. They are very active in saving the environment. We attend several good lectures together and share many liberal views.

I find myself in a period of spiritual renewal. I have applied to become an Oblate of the Abbey of St. Walburga. Years ago, when I was living in Pittsburgh, I went back to my former monastery, St. Vincent Archabbey, in Latrobe. The Archabbot was then Father Leopold, with whom I had worked 5 years as a moderator in the student dorms when I was still a member of that community. Since I had kept alive my Benedictine spirituality, I asked him if I could become an Oblate of St. Vincent. He told me that I had to return to the Roman Catholic orthodoxy. I refused to do so, since I was entrenched in the Anglican Communion. In contrast, I found that the former Abbess and the current Abbess of St. Walburga have a much more ecumenical approach. Anyone who is a Christian, no matter whether lay or ordained, no matter what denomination, male or female, is welcome to become an Oblate of that monastery. This became my good fortune when I was received officially as an Oblate of the Abbey of St. Walburga, on Sunday, October 26, 2014.

For my name as an Oblate of the Order of Saint Benedict, I chose that of Saint Anselm, whose moto was *Fides quaerens intellectum*, meaning "faith seeking intellectual understanding." That is what inspired all my intellectual pursuits, searching for the truth wherever I could find it.

Saint Anselm is famous for his "ontological argument for the existence of God. Addressing his monks he said that "God is the name of the most perfect being. As such, that name signifies all perfections, including existence. Therefore, God must exist." Thomas Aquinas rejected this proof, because it simply means that God must exist in the mind which conceives God. For Aquinas, a proof for existence must take its point of departure in the world. That is what the five Aquinas demonstrations of God's existence begin with observable evidence in the world: the five arguments from 1) the Unmoved Mover; 2) the first Cause; 3) Contingency; 4) Degrees of Perfection; 5) Teleology. Thomas, however, did not think these arguments prove really why God exists, but only why it is reasonable to think that God exists.

Another theory of Saint Anselm was that of the atonement theory. He borrowed from the

German Feudal system the notion that when a noble person is offended, the gravity of the offense is determined by the dignity of the person offended. Since God is an infinite being, any offense against God is infinite. Thus, only an infinite redeemer is required. Only Jesus could fulfill that requirement. Many contemporary theologians, however, reject that theory because it pictures God as an angry and abusive Father who sacrificed his Son for revenge. Instead, they prefer to think of God as "loving the world so much that he sent his Son into the world to redeem it."

It was for love, not for revenge.

Every morning I begin with Morning Prayer from the Episcopal Book of Common prayer, followed by the reading of one chapter of the French New Testament (in order not to forget my French) and the same chapter in Spanish. Then I read a section of the Rule of St Benedict, with commentaries in French, from Dom Delatte, former Abbot of Solesmes, and in English, by Sister Joan Chittister, from her Abbey in Erie, Pennsylvania. I meditate on these. Then I go to Chilson recreational center for physical exercises, after which I am hungry and eat breakfast. Once a month I meet with other Oblates of St Walburgha for prayer and discussion of the commentary of the Holy Rule by the former Abbess, Mother Maria-Thomas Beil.

After I had moved to Loveland, in 2002, very soon, I realized that without the income I had from teaching in Kentucky, plus what I received from being interim rector of a parish in Barboursville, a total of $60,000, I was in dire financial need. As long as I had that income, I could easily meet the monthly charges on my credit cards, which I had abused earlier. With Susan's income, although we shared all household expenses, I could manage very well; without her income, I was in trouble.

In 2003, I applied for bankruptcy. For this purpose, I asked Susan for a divorce, because I did not want her to be sued for my debts. She was very generous. For instance, in the last three years of our marriage, she received an extra $50,000 a year from an investment her former husband had made; she gave it all to various forms of charity. She had bailed me out from an earlier financial crunch.

The experience of bankruptcy was so traumatic for me that I experienced the greatest depression of my life. I thought I would lose everything and become homeless. I gave most of my books to the Loveland library and The Anthology Bookstore, buried all my academic degrees (2 bachelors; 4 masters, and 1 doctorate), all my certificates of distinction, and all my family albums in the landfill on Wilson Avenue. After seven years I was free of debts and now I am living within my budget. Although I am still separated from Susan, we are now good friends. She is now living in an independent living residence in Huntington, W.V. and very happy.

Soon, I was asked by Father Bill Bacon or St. Paul, Fort Collins, to offer lodging to a veteran of Iraq and Afghanistan. I received Jody Dowell; he lived with me for five years and was extremely helpful in solving many of my housekeeping problems. He became to me like an extra son. When he finally got married, at which I officiated, and moved out, I put my house for sale. It went on the market on Friday; on Saturday, three visitors; on Sunday, sold. Within a month I moved to Wexford, an independent living residence, where I now live and am very happy.

On May 11, 2013, at 5:46 pm, my son Michel was killed while bicycling in Lyons, Colorado. He was bicycling before supper. He usually bicycled between 100 and 200 miles a week. The SUV, which crushed him, was driven by a man who had complained to the city council about the increasing number of cyclists who crowded the streets of Lyons. He was arrested for driving under the influence of alcohol and going in the wrong direction. He was accused of vehicular homicide. I do not know what happened to him, but I forgive him.

With my Christian faith, I overcame the loss of my son Michel. He died prematurely, at the height of his career, of his physical and emotional life. I do not seek revenge, but reconciliation. I have learned a lot from Michel, which will guide me. Often he would tell me: "Dad, stand up straight, keep your head high." He was a perfect gentleman and very generous to those in need. He died in Christ. His funeral at St John's Episcopal Church, in Boulder, was perfect. Over 400 people in attendance, with family, friends, and admirers. I believe he is in Christ and saved. Joan, his mother, is now a Buddhist. She had bought a cemetery lot in Helena, Montana, when she was a Roman

Catholic, which she used to bury some of the ashes of Michel there. I have kept some of the ashes of Michel, which I will have buried with my own ashes when I die, in the columbarium of All Saints Episcopal Church. The main bulk of Michel`s ashes are kept by his widow, Carrie. As she lost her Roman Catholic faith when she was a student at Smith College, she does not believe in afterlife, and does not know what to do with the ashes. After the funeral I invited Carrie a couple of times for lunch and spoke about the disposal the ashes of Michel. Since then, she told me not to call her anymore; she said she has good friends in Boulder who understand her.

My youngest son, Pierre, was remarried to Jessica and had two daughters, McClain and Sydney. After they moved from Denver to Austin, Texas, they were divorced. Pierre works for Dell. His only account is NASA: the fourteen different sites in this country. He provides the Dell technology for their scientific endeavors. I have not seen him since he came to Boulder for the funeral of Michel. He gave to Joan his parcel of Michel's ashes to be buried in Montana.

I am now the assistant priest at All Saints Episcopal Church, six blocks from where I live. I assist every Sunday at the 10 o'clock Holy Eucharist service. Every Thursday morning at 7am, I officiate at the Holy Eucharist, followed by breakfast. Every Monday afternoon, I offer a program of prayer, reading of the weekly Gospel, and the showing of different videos, after which we entertain questions and discussion. Some of the videos I have shown so far are: The Gospel of Matthew; the Holy Land Revealed with Jodi Magness; The New Testament with Bart D. Ehrman; The First Days of Christianity; Jesus and the Gospels, with Luke Johnson; the History of Christianity up to the Reformation, with Luke Johnson; the History of Christianity in the Reformation Era, with Brad Gregory; The Lives of Great Christians, with William Cooke; the Great Churches, with William Cooke.

Lately, I read the autobiography of Roy Bourgeois and saw the video he made: Pink Smoke Over the Vatican (2913) Roy Bourgeois was a Marine who fought in Vietnam, where he witnessed some of the cruelties the Americans were doing: napalm bombing, destruction of the farmland, and massacre of children. Repelled by this cruelty, he retired from the Marines and joined a missionary order serving in Latin American. There, he witnessed the extreme poverty and the oppression of the dominant forces. These were supported by the American corporations who used the graduates of the School of the Americas in Georgia, to assassinate Christian missionaries who were supporting the poor. Father Bourgeois became an opponent of the School of "Assassins." He was offended by the oppression of women in the Catholic Church. Hence, his film entitled "Pink Smoke over the Vatican" which documents the controversial movement of women seeing to be ordained in the Roman Catholic Church. On June 3rd, 2008, the Congregation for the Doctrine of the Faith issued a sweeping order of excommunication for "the crime of attempting sacred ordination of a woman. " Pink Smoke Over the Vatican" chronicles the events that led up to this severe punishment. It tells the stories of the determined women and men who, through the forbidden and illicit path of female ordination, are working to end the underlying misogyny and outdated feudal governance that is slowly destroying the Roman Catholic Church.

Ordination of Women in the Roman Catholic Church

Already in 1963, when I decided to leave the Roman Church and become an Episcopalian, I realized that I was not leaving the Catholic Church, but only the Roman sectarian segment of the Catholic Church, which in includes the Anglican Communion of which the Episcopalian Church is a member. The fact that women were excluded from voice and vote at Vatican II while they were given voice and vote at the World Anglican Congress was symbolic for me of the excommunication of women from full participation in the Roman sectarian establishment.

Since then, both the biography of Father Roy Bourgeois, <u>My Journey from Silence to solidarity: Why a Catholic priest for 40 years was expelled from the priesthood</u> and the film, <u>Pink Smoke Over the Vatican</u> have confirmed my decision to leave a denomination that has lost its monopoly of the Catholicity (universality) of the Church. In November 2008, the Vatican's Congregation for the Doctrine of the Faith ordered Bourgeois to recant his public support of women priests and refrain from further advocacy. He responded that to recant would be a betrayal of his conscience. In 1968, Archbishop Joseph Ratzinger, later Pope Benedict XVI, wrote a commentary on a key Vatican II document, <u>Gaudium et Spes</u>. He wrote: "Over the pope...there still stands one's own conscience, which must be obeyed before all else, if necessary against the requirement of ecclesiastical authority." In the 13th century, the great Thomas Aquinas had already written that if your conscience tells you that if the Roman Church teaches something that is against your conscience, you have a moral obligation to leave it.

After his expulsion from Maryknoll community and the priesthood for believing that women are also called to the priesthood, Roy Bourgois wrote: "They cannot dismiss the issue of gender equality in the Catholic Church. The demand for gender equality is rooted in justice and dignity and will not go away. .. The exclusion of women from the priesthood is a grave injustice against women, our Church, and our loving God, who calls both men and women to be priests. When there is an injustice silence is the voice of complicity. My conscience compelled me to break my silence and addressed the sin of sexism in my Church. "

In March 2013, New York Times/CBS poll reported that 70% of Catholics in the USA believe that Pope Francis should allow women to be priests. While over 4,000 priests have abused over 10,000 children at the cost of over $1.2 billion, none of these priests and bishops who protected them, have been excommunicated. Anyone who promotes priesthood for women is automatically excommunicated by the Vatican. That is an injustice that cries to heaven.

"In the current heated discussions about women in ministry," Walter Brueggemann wrote in one of his books, The Bible Makes Sense, "it is important not to lose sight of the redefinitions of power that may be offered to us in this struggle. It may be that God is calling the church to abandon hierarchical, coercive forms of power for the sake of vulnerable power that stands with and suffers alongside. We do not yet know what such power would mean, but clearly it means a sharp reorientation, for Jesus is judged by the world to be utterly powerless, and yet he did in deed have the only power that mattered."

Liberation Theology

I read also several books dealing with the Liberation movement in Latin America. Starting with Harvey Cox, <u>The Silencing of Leonardo Boff (1988), I</u> continued with Gustavo Gutierrez, <u>A Theology of Liberation</u>. Gutierrez is a native of Peru, was educated in Lima, Chile, and at Louvain, in Belgium He lives and works among the poor of Rimac, a Lima slum. Professor of Theology at The Catholic University, he is author of several books: <u>On Job: God-Talk and the Suffering of the Innocent; the Power of the Poor in History; We drink from Our Own Wells; The Truth Shall make You Free; and Las casas: In Search of the Poor of Jesus Christ.</u>

<u>A Theology of Liberation</u> is a classic of Liberation in which he reviews the history of Christian theology up to its incarnation in the Latin American Church. It offers also some perspectives the future of the Christian mystery. He concludes with a remark from Pascal and writes: "All political theologies, the theologies of hope, of revolution, and of liberation, are not worth one act of genuine solidarity with exploited social classes. They are not worth one act of faith, love, and hope, committed – in one way of another – in active participation to liberate

humankind from everything that dehumanizes it and prevents it from living according to the will of the Father."

I enjoyed immensely reading Leonardi Boff: Jesus Christ Liberator. He reviews the history of the scientific and critical studies of Scripture to propose a new Critical Christology for our time. "The liberation involved here has to do with economic, social, political, and ideological structures...It takes the side of the oppressed, feeling that it is compelled to do this by its faith in the historical Jesus. ``

In our present historical situation, non-commitment would signify acceptance of the existing situation and subtle stand in favor of those already favored." The liberation theology elaborated from the point of view of Latin America stresses the historical Jesus over the Christ of faith, because it sees a structural similarity between the situations in Jesus' day and those in our own time; because the historical Jesus puts us in direct contact with his liberative praxis which fosters a critique of humanity and society as they appear historically... systematically speaking, we can say that the historical Jesus did not preach about himself or the church or God but rather about the kingdom of God."

Boff prefers to speak of orthopraxis more than orthodoxy, thus liberating human practice from necrophilic structures. The historical Jesus opposed using power to impose the will of God. He chose to die rather than to implant the kingdom of God by violence. "His call for conversion, his new image of God, his freedom toward sacred traditions, and his prophetic criticism of those holding political, economic, and religious power combined to provoke the conflict that resulted in his violent death. "The theology of liberation, of Jesus Christ the Liberator, is the pain-filled cry of oppressed Christians." The problem in Latin America emerged originally because most the bishops came from the ruling class and supported the status quo. Now, since Mendellin, the situation has changed. Most of the Latin American bishops, like the present Pope, Francis, have been influenced by the Liberation theology.

The best introduction to <u>Liberation Theology</u> is that provided by the two brothers: Leonardo and Clodovis Boff, originally in 1986, and reprinted in 2012.

They speak of three stages: seeing, judging, acting.

First comes the socio-analytical (or historico-analytical) stage: finding out why the oppressed are oppressed;

Secondly, the hermeneutical stage: trying to discern what God's plan is for the poor;

thirdly, the practical stage operates in the sphere of action: how to overcome oppression in accordance with God's plan. There is racist, ethnic, and sexual oppression. The poor are the disfigured Son of God, the suffering servant, the persecuted

The biblical books favored by liberation theology are:

Exodus: the epic of the politico-religious liberation   of   a   mass   of slaves

Prophets: denunciation of injustices, vindication of the rights of the poor

Wisdom: divine revelation contained in popular wisdom

Gospels: liberating actions of Jesus: his actions, death and resurrection

Acts of the Apostles: the ideal of free   and   liberating   Christian community;

Liberation theology also finds inspiration in the individual evangelical experiences of so many saints and prophets, many of them declared heretics at the time, but whose liberating impact can clearly be seen today - Francis of Assisi, Savonarola, Meister Eckhart, Catherine of Sienna, Barolome de Las Casas. The key themes of Liberation theology are: Solidarity with the poor: worshiping God and Communing with Christ. There are theological motivation (on God`s part); Christological motivation (on Christ`s part) apostolic motivation (on the part of the Apostles. The living God sides with the oppressed against the pharaohs of this world; the kingdom is God`s project in history and eternity; Jesus, the Son of God took on oppression in order to set us free.

Recently, I read a good article in Sojourners, (April 2015), by Emilie Teresa Smith, an Argentine-Canadian Anglican priest, on Pope Francis' efforts to restore Roman relations with Latin American liberation theologians. She wrote: ``The popes of the 1980 and `90s removed all support for the promoters of liberation theology who had lived with a preferential option for the poor, born from

Vatican II and the 1968 Medellin conference of Latin American bishops. The church`s identification with the poor was a direct strike against the closed oligarchic structures that had strangled the lands and peoples since the European conquest. The oligarchy which controlled governments and armies, struck back. The Latin American oligarchic wars created countless liberation Christian martyrs.

Efforts toward recognizing the Christian martyrs and saints of the wars were blocked by church officials. Soon conservative church hierarchs were again ascendant. The six instructors of the University of Central America – Sobrino`s brother Jesuits – their housekeeper, and her daughter who were brutally murdered by members of the U.S.-backed Salvadoran military were not recognized in any category as protectors of the faith. The murdered bishops of Latin America – including Enrique Angelelli of Argentina (1976), Juan José Gerardi of Guatemala (1998), and Oscar Romero of El Salvador (1980) – were left out of the list of nearly 500 saints proclaimed by Pope John Paul II.`

Additionally, Liberation theologians were disowned and prevented from writing. The Vatican`s doctrinal office, then headed by Cardinal Joseph Ratzinger (who became Pope Benedict XVI), condemned liberation theology for its supposed "serious ideological deviations." Theologian Leonardo was silenced in 1985. Peruvian Gustavo Gutierrez, called the father of liberation theology, was censured. Even Sobrino was notified by the Vatican that disciplinary measures were under way against his theological and doctrinal teaching.

But with the arrival of Pope Francis, a fresh wind is blowing. Almost immediately, Francis set about restoring relations with Latin American liberation theologians. Boff and Gutierrez have both met with the pontiff, while Sobrino speaks of "Papa Francisco" with his usual caution – hopeful, slightly ironic, infinitely patient.

The greatest sign that Pope Francis is doing something different came on Feb. 2, when the Vatican office that promotes individuals for sainthood declared that El Salvador`s assassinated Archbishop Romero was officially a martyr of the church, that his murder had been an act of hatred for the faith.

This is more than a fine canonical point. It is a remarkable statement, vindicating the courageous death of many other martyrs. Those who killed them would have firmly called themselves Christians. The Vatican has (at last) proclaimed that they were in fact not Christians at all, but were enemies of the faith.

Recently, I read an article of Cardinal Walter Kaspar on "How Pope Francis sees the church." He quotes Pope Francis: "In reference to the conversion in pastoral care, I would like to remind you that "pastoral care" is nothing other than the exercise of the church's motherhood. She gives birth, breastfeeds, lets grow, corrects, nourishes, leads by the hand…here is need therefore for a church that is capable of rediscovering the womb of mercy. Without mercy it is scarcely possible today to penetrate into a world of the "injured" who need understanding, forgiveness, and love… Laypeople are, put simply, the vast majority of the people of God. The minority – ordained ministers – are at their service. "

Yet, the women are over 51% of the people of God, with no voice and no vote. Cardinal Kaspar adds: "All the same, the reservation of the priesthood to men, as a sign of Christ, the bridegroom who offers himself in the Eucharist, is not open to discussion."

[To promote priesthood for women ends in an excommunication. This is an exercise of the power of domination, not the power of service]

"The church should be an open house with open doors," wrote Kaspar. The pope has laid the groundwork for allowing Christians in irregular situations, such as divorced and remarried individuals, after examination of their respective situations, to the sacraments of reconciliation and Eucharist. I well remember that when I was a Roman Catholic priest I was not allowed to offer the sacraments to either the divorced and remarried individuals, nor to anyone using contraception methods. For Pope Francis, the guiding star of evangelization and of this kind of pastoral care is Mary, Jesus's mother- and our mother. Mary is the subject of *Evangelii gaudium*. "Without Mary the church would lack a feminine image."

What about 51% of the Catholic population who are women! Are they not able to provide that feminine image? The only reason why Pope Francis cannot change his mind on the priestly ordination of women is, to my mind, his reluctance to challenge the concept of infallibility, which would suggest that earlier popes were mistaken in denying the possibility of woman priesthood. I was tempted, at this point, to say something nasty about the Pope.

Then I remembered a passage from the primeval history in Genesis 9:20-27: "Noah... drank some of the wine and became drunk, and he lay uncovered in his tent. And Ham, the father of Canaan, saw the nakedness of his father, and told his two brothers outside. Then Shem and Japheth took a garment, laid it on both their shoulders, and walked backward and discovered the nakedness of their father; their faces were turned away, and they did not see their father's nakedness. When Noah awoke from his wine and knew what his youngest son had done to him, he said, "Cursed be Canaan; lowest of slaves shall he be to his brothers." He also said, "Blessed by the Lord my God be Shem; and let Canaan be his slave. May God make space for Japheth, and let him live in the tents of Shem; and Canaan be his slave."

According to the critical editor, "This passage describes Noah's curse upon Canaan. In the new age, Noah was the first to engage in agriculture. His success fulfilled the prophecy made at his birth. Since the curse was later put on Canaan rather than on Ham, it is likely that Canaan was the actor originally. Here Noah's youngest son is clearly Canaan, not Ham. Curse implies that Canaan's subjugation to Israel was the result of Canaanite sexual practices. The last verse may refer to the Philistines, one of the sea-peoples who dwelt in the tents of Shem, i.e. conquered the coast of Canaan."

For Sobrino, liberation theology, no matter what it is called, is the inevitable moving of the Holy Spirit, God's unstoppable renovation of the whole creation. San Romero de las Americas, is already a saint in the hearts of the people. He has been for 35 years. The people in El Salvador, in Latin America, and around the world have declared this to be God's truth, no matter what is said thousands of miles away in Rome."

Recently, I have been reading Henri Nouwen, <u>Discernment</u>, in which he visited and recognized the tragic political, economic, military, and religious conflicts in Nicaragua, Guatemala, and Peru, many of them involving the church and government. When he returned to the USA, he remarked that what the U.S. government and, indirectly, the U.S. people are doing in Central America is unjust, illegal, and immoral. He wrote: "It is unjust because we intervene in a country that in no way threatens us; it is illegal because we break every existing international law against intervention in an autonomous country' and it is immoral because we inflict destruction, torture, and death on innocent people. Christ is risen means that we are a people of reconciliation, not of division; people of love, not of hate; people of life, not of death."

Lately, on November 5, 2014, while sitting in All Saints Episcopal Church, in Loveland, for the service of Holy Eucharist, I experienced my first heart attack. Since then, many medical examinations have been performed and the results were very good. The doctor said she would see me in six months. That was just an alert. Still, my hearing problem deprives me from enjoying conversations with my friends.

My creed includes the notion of *pan-en-theism*, the belief that God is in everything and everything is in God. This is not pantheism, which means that everything is God. It maintains both transcendence of divinity over everything as well as the immanence of divinity within everything. In the Acts of the Apostles.17: 27-28, Paul speaking to the Greeks in Athens quotes two Greek stoic philosophers, Epimenides and Cilicia: "For in him we live and move and have our being...for we too are his offspring."

From my biblical studies I assert that the historical Jesus became the Christ of Faith by his resurrection. The resurrection is not a physical resuscitation of the body, but a spiritual transformation which can be perceived only by faith. I recognize the intellectual probity of the scholars of the Westar Institute, but with the added advantage of faith by those biblical scholars who are believers. The incarnation means that God assumed all of humanity in humility, in a crib, not on a royal throne; it means that both man and woman have equal rights in the kingdom of God. The disciples were chosen neither for their wisdom nor for their power. The early Church was for the *anawim*, the poor of

Yahweh. The early Church was persecuted for three hundred years until the conversion of Constantine. From then on, the Christians, under the influence of Augustine's theory of the "just war" it became destroyers of heretics. Jesus had said "Love your enemies;" after Constantine, Christians said: "Destroy the heretics."

Later on, the <u>Decretals</u> conceived in the 9th century by the lawyers of the Pope, but declared ``false`` by the humanists in the 16th century, assumed that Constantine had given to the bishop of Rome the imperial power along with his spiritual power. We must remember that the Emperor Constantine was still the Supreme Pontiff of the Roman pagan religion when he convened and presided over the Nicean Council of 325. The False Decretals of Isidore reinforced the power of the Bishop of Rome against the Patriarch of Constantinople, which led to the Eastern Schism between the Roman and the Orthodox Churches

In his history of <u>Medieval Christianity</u>, Kevin Madigan quotes a chronicler's description of Boniface VIII's reception in 1298 of the ambassadors of the claimants to the imperial throne "Sitting on a throne, wearing on his head the diadem of Constantine, his right hand on the hilt of the sword with which he was girt, he{the pope} cried out: "Am I not the supreme pontiff? Is this throne not the pulpit of Peter? Is it not my duty to watch over the rights of the Empire? It is I who am Caesar, It is I who am emperor.``

On the basis of the false donation of Constantine, in 1302, Boniface VIII issued the bull Unam Sanctam which historians regard as the most extreme claim of papal supremacy. The abuse of papal authority led to the quest of power and, in the 14th century, to the situation when there was three popes, for political reasons, all claiming spiritual authority. The Council of Constance tried to remedy the situation by establishing the authority of the council over the pope, since the three popes could not agree. Obviously, none of them was infallible. Very soon, however, the next council dominated by the pope reestablished the primacy of the bishop of Rome, which led eventually to Vatican I when Pope Pius IX declared himself infallible, "even without the church." These are the very words of the definition. For me, that was the height of arrogance equal to the saying of King Louis XIV: "I am the State."``

John XXIII tried to restore the collegiality of bishops, but soon John Paul II restored papal primacy. Now Francis has given up the pride of papal primacy, returning to the warning of Jesus to the apostles, not to become seekers of power but servants of the people. The new trends can be seen in <u>The Emergent Christ</u>, by Ilia Delio, in <u>The Emerging Christianity</u>, by Phyllis Tickle, <u>A Generous Orthodoxy,</u> by Brian McClaren, and <u>The Left Hand of God</u>, by Michael Lerner.

I believe in an ecumenical Catholicism like Brian McClaren who calls for a radical, Christ-centered orthodoxy of faith and practice in a missional, generous spirit. My old professor at Yale, Hans Frei, coined the term *generous orthodoxy* to describe an understanding of Christianity that includes elements of both liberal and conservative elements.

On Michael Lerner's book, Jim Wallis has written: "Lerner's rare and eloquent voice goes beyond left/right political dichotomies, will help progressives overcome their fear of spirituality and will challenge spiritual people to avoid the dangers of narcissistic self-indulgence." Lerner wrote: "The premise of the Left Hand of God is that we have a common interest in caring for everyone in our society—that each of us flourishes when we all thrive emotionally, spiritually, economically, intellectually, culturally, and physically. One natural sequence of such mutuality is a deep and immediate responsibility to build a world based on justice, equality, fairness, and peace, a world that cares for the well-being of everyone in the planet."

The long collaboration of the Church with temporal
power often led to its persecution of reformers, even during our lifetime. Witness the priest-workers in France and the Liberation theologians in South America! I still believe in the freedom of conscience and the freedom of intellectual work, so well demonstrated by the work of Hans Kueng.

I believe also in the renewal of spiritual life, exemplified by the works of Thomas Merton and Thomas Keating . Merton was a Trappist monk of the Abbey of Gethsemani, in Kentucky. He was a poet, social activist, and student of comparative religion. He pioneered dialogue with prominent Asian spiritual figures, including the Dalai Lama, the Japanese writer D.T. Suzuki, the Thai Buddhist monk Buddhadasa, and the

Vietnamese monk Thich Nhat Hanh. He died in Cambodia where he was campaigning for the end of the war in Vietnam. He was electrocuted coming out of a shower; a rumor ran that he was killed by the CIA.

Keating is a Trappist monk and priest, once the Abbot of St.Joseph`s monastery in Spencer, Massachussets. There he invited a Buddhist monk to teach his monks on the various methods of meditation. Then, he moved to St. Benedict`s Abbey, in Snow Mass, Colorado, where he teaches Centering prayer. Buddhist monks were welcome to pray with Catholic monks, until Bishop Chaput of Denver threatened to suspend the Abbot Boyle for this "offense" to Roman Catholic exclusivity.

For me, the Benedictine spirituality is my way to salvation, which I pursue as an Oblate of St. Walbugha. My former Scripture professor, Father Demetrius Dumm, wrote an excellent book, <u>Cherish Christ Above All: The Bible in the Rule of Benedict</u>. At the end of his Holy Rule, Benedict wrote: "What page, what passage of the inspired books of the Old and New Testaments is not the truest of guides for human life." Father Dumm considers the historical-critical method is the indispensable method for the scientific study of the meaning of ancient texts.

Two books that clarified my thinking were the French-Canadian Ursuline sister, Cecile Dionne, who is also a psychoanalytical therapist and wrote an excellent book, Oser la Rencountre: Foi et Psychalanyse (Dare the encounter: faith and psychoanalysis). The other is Dieu Immediat (God immediately) by Eugen Drewermann. This includes a dialogue between Gewedoline Jarcsyk, a philosopher and journalist with Drewermann, a Roman Catholic theologian of Paderborn, who has been silenced by the Roman Curia for reading the Bible and Church history through psychoanalysis. He contests the intermediaries between God and man by the dogma, the Church as an institution, the clerical power contrary to the gospel, closed in its whole to the discovery of depth psychology. He proposes that Christian mysticism is the best way to encounter God, as well as the central prayer technique taught by Father Thomas Keating.

The hospitality often associated with the Benedictines begins with the belief of God's presence by quiet, trusting prayer and the practice of Christian discipline, intended more for exposing and eliminating illusions than imposing order. The prologue of the Rule ends with these words: "Do not be daunted immediately by fear and run away from the road that leads to salvation. It is bound to be narrow at the outset. But as we progress in this way of life and in faith, we shall run on the path of God`s commandments, our hearts overflowing with the inexpressible delight of love."

When I review my life, the monastic vows made at St. Benoit-du-Lac and renewed at Saint Vincent Archabbey, then, broken when I became an Episcopalian, I certainly feel a certain amount of guilt, even though I rationalized that. Then, after three marriages and three divorces, I do not seem to be able to maintain any marital stability in my life. I know and believe
that God is a prodigal Father and has forgiven me. I have peace in my soul and feel beloved by God. I have always remained attached to the Rule of Saint Benedict, even when I have been unfaithful to it.

Dear Lord, my Savior, have compassion on me, a sinner, repentant but redeemed. Amen.

Acknowledgments

I wish to acknowledge first all the members of my family for their encouragement and nurturing as I was growing up physically, mentally, and spiritually, especially my Mother whose vow at my baptism predestined me for a life of priesthood. I am grateful to the Oblates of Mary Immaculate who administered the prep school, the liberal arts college, the Institute of Philosophy, and the medical school where I first received such good instruction and inspiration. Then, the Abbot and the monks of Saint Benoit-du-Lac, where I was formed in the spirituality of Saint Benedict, are to be thanked. Then, the Archabbot and monks of Saint Vincent Archabbey, in Latrobe, Pennsylvania, provided me the opportunity to exercise an intellectual ministry for which I was well trained. Bishop Anselm Phelps-Stokes, Bishop of the Episcopal Diocese of Massachusetts, accepted me in the Episcopal Church, provided a favorable environment for the development of my intellectual and spiritual development. The faculty and professors of the Graduate School of

Religious Studies at Yale University created a most inspiring milieu for the nurturing of serious academic studies.

Then, I wish to express my grateful appreciation for all the Roman Catholic, Anglican, and scholars of other denominations, who by their teaching and books stimulated my curiosity to maintain as much as possible an intellectual integrity in searching for Truth. I have quoted from those who inspired me the most. I thank also the previous Mother Abbess Marie-Thomas and the current Mother Abbess Marie-Michael, of St. Walburgha, who received me as an Oblate of Saint Benedict.

I wish to thank Marie-Alice McComb for her sponsorhip.

Finally, I wish to thank especially Charlotte Hinger, a scholarly historian and published author, who guided me in the publication of this manuscript.

Postscript

<u>Apology for a Monk in the World</u> is the fascinating story of Jean-Jacques D'Aoust, a priest, a scholar and a man. A story of love and loss, of triumph and failure. A story of one man's struggler to be a man of God and a man in the world. It's been my privilege to get to know JJ the past 5 years. By reading this book you get to know this wonderful man too.

Rick Parker, Retired businessman and Senior Warden of All Saints Episcopal Church, 2012-2014.

Made in the USA
San Bernardino, CA
11 July 2015